DRESSAGE MASTERS

DRESSAGE MASTERS

TECHNIQUES AND PHILOSOPHIES OF FOUR LEGENDARY TRAINERS

KLAUS BALKENHOL
ERNST HOYOS
DR. UWE SCHULTEN-BAUMER
GEORGE THEODORESCU

DAVID COLLINS

The Lyons Press
Guilford, Connecticut
An imprint of The Globe Pequot Press

To buy books in quantity for corporate use
or incentives, call **(800) 962–0973, ext. 4551,**
or e-mail **premiums@GlobePequot.com**.

Copyright © 2006 by David Collins

ALL RIGHTS RESERVED. No part of this book may be reproduced or transmitted in any form by any means, electronic or mechanical, including photocopying and recording, or by any information storage and retrieval system, except as may be expressly permitted in writing from the publisher. Requests for permission should be addressed to The Lyons Press, Attn: Rights and Permissions Department, P.O. Box 480, Guilford, CT 06437.

The Lyons Press is an imprint of The Globe Pequot Press.

10 9 8 7 6 5 4 3 2 1

Printed in the United States of America

ISBN-13: 978-159228-674-4
ISBN-10: 1-59228-674-7

The Library of Congress Cataloging-in-Publication data is available on file.

"... and he whispered
to the horse,
trust no man in
whose eyes
you do not see
yourself reflected
as an equal."

UNKNOWN

Dedication

This book is dedicated to an animal to which we owe nothing less than our entire civilization.

Our rapid journey down the path to technological prowess is owed to speedy hoofprints which saved many trudging footprints. Due to the horse's spirit, honesty, and strength our ancestors rode high on a sturdy back. The wings of the horse enabled mankind to fly well above a quagmire of lethal human frailty. In homage to this archetypal animal, may our dedication to understanding the art of dressage brighten the future of each young horse.

DRESSAGE MASTERS

TABLE OF CONTENTS

ACKNOWLEDGMENTS VIII
INTRODUCTION IX

CHAPTER ONE — KLAUS BALKENHOL
BRIEF BIO 2
GENERAL QUESTIONS 3
TRAINING QUESTIONS 27
    YOUNG HORSE 27
    COLLECTION 35

CHAPTER TWO — ERNST HOYOS
BRIEF BIO 52
GENERAL QUESTIONS 54
TRAINING QUESTIONS 73
    YOUNG HORSE 73
    COLLECTION 76

CHAPTER THREE — DR. UWE SCHULTEN-BAUMER
BRIEF BIO 86
GENERAL QUESTIONS 89
TRAINING QUESTIONS 97
    YOUNG HORSE 97
    COLLECTION 99

CHAPTER FOUR — GEORGE THEODORESCU
BRIEF BIO 110
GENERAL QUESTIONS 112
TRAINING QUESTIONS 133
    YOUNG HORSE 133
    COLLECTION 136

ACKNOWLEDGMENTS

When envisioning the modern, stereotypical writer, one imagines a person in a self-inflicted state of solitary confinement; he is hunched over a keyboard, at odd hours, pecking letters onto a screen with nimble fingers. There is more than a grain of truth in this image (except, in my case, the part about the nimble fingers). Writing is a solo task, but all writers owe thanks to many people who made their endeavor possible.

Accordingly, I would first like to thank my partner, Anni de Saint Phalle, for her dedicated help, encouragement, and support. Judith Balkenhol planned and scheduled most of the interviews, which was a most difficult task. She also lent a hand with the editing of Klaus Balkenhol's chapter. Grace Lee assisted with the majority of the travel. She made this book possible. Daniela Domnick helped edit and select photos for the Ernst Hoyos chapter. Next, I owe much to author Barbara Lang Stern, who encouraged and supported my efforts in this undertaking. She and Liz Spiwack helped form the initial concept behind this book. Author Scott Tilldman and my agent Susan Barry made getting a contract possible, and the staff at the Authors Guild was most helpful during negotiations. *Dressage Today* magazine editor Patricia Lasko was very encouraging during my initial forays into writing articles, which led to writing this book. I would also like to thank many people, including my friends, students, and business associates who have been understanding and accommodating during my absences. Last, but not least, I would like to thank my editor, Steven Price, whose suggestions helped to shape this book.

Of course, I owe thanks to busy dressage masters who made time for interviews and discussions. Their names and stories follow.

INTRODUCTION

THE ORIGINAL OBJECTIVE FOR THIS BOOK WAS TO SHARE A SMALL AMOUNT OF CRITICAL KNOWLEDGE FROM TWELVE OF THE GREATEST DRESSAGE MASTERS OF OUR TIME. That plan succumbed early to the sheer volume of useful material. The breadth and depth of interesting and valuable knowledge from the first four interviewees made further edits too painful—there was just too much good stuff. Additional inspiration for a smaller-scale book came from the fact that each of these individuals says his knowledge and understanding is constantly increasing—each remains committed to learning and evolving under the guidance of the best riding teacher of all, the horse. Two of these masters are still passionate and productive in dressage at age eighty; they are a true source of inspiration.

In the following 146 pages (including 182 photographs), these masters share a few of their key points of wisdom, including valuable glimpses into their philosophies and paradigms, which have evolved as they achieved their considerable success. These four trainers are responsible for significant contributions to the training and teaching of horses and riders that together won an incredible 90 percent of the Olympic dressage gold medals in the last four Olympic Games. During this period, the German dressage squads won eighteen out of the twenty Individual and Team Gold Medals awarded. This is an unprecedented achievement in the history of equestrian sports—a 90 percent win record in a sport/art in which very few countries have won even one of these coveted prizes. These few masters have taught

Much of Germany is comprised of adjacent agricultural and industrial areas.

students who won more gold medals than entire nations—Sweden ranks behind Germany in the gold medal count with a total of seven, followed by the USSR with four. Other countries that have won gold medals are France, Switzerland, the Netherlands, and Austria. (German jumper riders are also well known for a system of training that is based on dressage. This is a major contributing factor to their success. German jumping squads hold the record for most Olympic show jumping gold medals.)

The most important aspect of the great masters' successes, for the purposes of this book, lies in their uncanny abilities to produce successful horse and rider pairs—to communicate

Young horses in Germany at a top breeding farm. How many future champions are here in such humble beginnings? The horses spend most days out on the fields. At night they become "socialized" by living in close proximity to other foals.

their knowledge to others. Great trainers, great instructors, and great riders are three separate but related categories. Often, success in one does not guarantee success in another. These masters are the people who stand behind the scenes at world-class competitions. They help others to achieve success.

Curious is the fact that these great masters—two native Germans, one Romanian, and one Austrian—live within a small circle of the world; it has a radius of less than a hundred miles. As a successful restaurateur once said, "I always build my restaurants right next to successful restaurants. Together we create a dining district, a place for people to come. The worst scenario is to be in the middle of nowhere, alone." This small area of the world is rich in equestrian tradition and knowledge. It possesses an unusual mixture of industrial and agricultural areas in close proximity, which provide land and money to support the breeding of quality horses. Perhaps most important, the culture respects and idolizes the horse.

The fact that the featured masters are all male may seem odd in a sport that is increasingly dominated by females. However, this recent trend started in the 1980s. Before then, the top ranks of the dressage world were predominately men, most likely a result of the military tradition behind dressage. As the current cadre of riders matures, most future great masters will be female, as exemplified by Kyra Kyrkland.

Of course, a critic could search for and probably find faults with some of the riders pictured in this book. After all, most Grand Prix classes can be won with a 75 percent. In school this would only earn an average grade; the difficult sport of dressage can always be performed better. However, judging by the success of these masters, they must be doing a lot of things right. Therefore, any mistakes of these students or horses must be judged in context to the level of excellence of the masters, the Yin and the Yang of their distinction. Therefore, analyzing faults would not be a good teaching tool, since these mistakes haven't interfered with success. You can watch any rider if you want to see mistakes. If you ever have the pleasure of watching any of the people in these pictures ride, focus on what they do right. A person who looks solely for mistakes searches for a guiding image in a house of mirrors, a form of solidity in a myriad of refractions and reflections. A person who searches for positive aspects that contributed to a master's success often discovers a beacon to light the darkness.

There are many others who could have been included in this book, but time and space are limited, and their omission is not intended as disrespect.

KLAUS BALKENHOL

Brief Bio

Klaus Balkenhol entered the dressage world in 1977, when he made a phone call to the German National Equestrian Center in Warendorf and asked to be included in a training session for Grand Prix riders. At that time he was thirty-eight years old and worked as a mounted police officer in Düsseldorf. He was unknown as a dressage rider. Perhaps out of politeness, the authorities at Warendorf agreed. (Who wants to be on the bad side of a police officer?) They were in for a surprise. At the end of the training session, Willi Schultheis, who was then coach of the German team, said Klaus Balkenhol and his mount Rabauke should be ranked in the top eight horse and rider pairs in Germany. In 1979, Klaus Balkenhol and Rabauke were reserve champions at the German Finals.

Klaus Balkenhol rode Rabauke to many more victories at the national level in Germany. However, his next Grand Prix horse, Goldstern, would bring Balkenhol international fame. At the 1992 Barcelona Olympics, Klaus Balkenhol received the individual bronze medal and was a part of the gold medal German team. In the 1996 Olympics in Atlanta, he won another team gold. Additionally, Mr. Balkenhol won the individual silver medal and a team gold at the 1994 World Equestrian Games in The Hague.

After his considerable success as an individual rider, Mr. Balkenhol coached the German Olympic team for the 2000 Olympic Games in Australia. He worked with gold medal team riders Isabell Werth, Nadine Capellmann-Biffar, Ulla Salzgeber, and Alexandra Simmons de Ridder. At the Sydney Games, Isabel won the individual silver medal, and Ulla was the individual bronze medalist. At the World Equestrian Games in 1998, he taught the individual gold medalist and the gold medal winning team.

In 2001 Klaus Balkenhol was hired by the United States Equestrian Team (USET) as a dressage coach and technical advisor. Under his guidance, the United States achieved unprecedented results, a silver medal for the team at the 2002 World Equestrian Games in Jerez, Spain (where Mr. Balkenhol also coached the individual gold medalist, his long-time student Nadine Capellmann). The United States also won the Olympic team bronze at Athens in 2004 under Mr. Balkenhol's supervision.

General Questions

Why do you ride?

I started to ride before I could walk. My parents put me on horses. I rode both sport horses and work horses, the warmbloods that were used in the fields. I grew up on a farm not far from here. One of my first experiences with passage came with riding these work horses. After being in the fields all day, they were anxious to get home. I would get on them, ride them back to the barn, and they really wanted to go. At the time, I didn't know what they were doing, but I realized later that they were passaging.

As a child, I joined a local "Reitverein," or riding club. I competed at the lower levels in dressage and jumping and eventing. The local economy was depressed for farming so, at the age of twenty, I joined the police force and moved to Düsseldorf. There, I joined that local riding club. At the age of twenty-four, I met Judith at that riding club. We shared a love of horses. About five years later, we married. In Düsseldorf, I worked as a mounted police officer. I have been involved with horses my whole life.

I was fortunate when I went to police training. I had the opportunity to train with a real artist, the last of a generation of cavalry officers. My teacher was a man named Otto Hartwich from the old cavalry school. He required that the horses be trained to "L" level in all disciplines. (The "L" level in Germany translates roughly as follows: Dressage, 2nd Level; Jumping, 1.20 meters or 4'; Three-Day Eventing, Training Level). It's too bad that it is not the same today, but we don't have teachers like that anymore.

Otto was an artist. He could put power and technique into a horse and make it beautiful. He understood how to develop a horse's body and mind. All of the horses just got normal food, and they never seemed to get sick. We rarely called a vet. Yes, we breed better horses today. They are more athletic and easier to ride. They are really bred for the sport. But Otto taught normal horses to levade, to piaffe, to courbette. He was a beautiful jumper rider. He and Georg Wahl, the trainer of the Swiss Olympic gold medalist Christine Stückleberger, were colleagues. Otto didn't like to compete. He practiced his art quietly and trained the police horses.

(It is interesting to note that Klaus Balkenhol achieved his first fame on two police horses: Rabauke, a top international Grand Prix horse, and Goldstern, a top Olympic Grand Prix horse. Their purchase prices were 4,000DM and 6,000DM respectively—roughly $2,000 and $3,000. This is an unprecedented achievement in modern dressage. However, horse dealers out there should take heart. The more expensive horse did win more.)

What makes a good rider?

One who understands the horse. One who is capable of listening to the horse. You have to speak their language. When you ride, you have to know what this horse will allow or tolerate, and more important, what they won't tolerate.

A good rider is one who understands the half halt. The rider has to close the hand and slow the horse, but then *immediately* release with the hand. If a rider holds too long, he pulls the horse onto the forehand, he blocks the energy from behind, and he creates rhythm faults. This is especially true if the rider holds and drives at the same time. All of the energy that the rider creates pushes the horse onto the forehand. A rider has to activate the hind end of the horse *only when the horse is light in the hand*; the rider must strive to drive the horse forward only when the horse is not

Figure 1.1

Anabel Balkenhol on her eight-year-old horse, Little Big Man, demonstrates the ultimate product of successful half halts, the piaffe. Note the steady and light contact with the horse's mouth. Her legs drive only as necessary; otherwise they hang loosely at the horse's sides. The muscles of the horse are working but not tense. The topline muscles show particularly good development. The hind feet are beginning to develop consistent suspension as this young horse gains strength in his back and hindquarters.

pulling. A rider must explain to the horse that he must work more without running forward against the hand. In this way the horse will relax in its back and maintain a nice, even rhythm.

What makes a good trainer?

One who has a good understanding of dressage theory, and one who can execute the theory on a practical level. He has to be able to place himself into the situation in which the student finds himself and successfully solve the problems. He has to be able to do this not only by riding the horse, but he also has to be able to explain to the student so the student understands how to do this on their own. A trainer has to give clear instructions. Above all, he has to think of what is in the best interest of the horse.

Figure 1.2

Klaus Balkenhol observes his students in the warm-up at the Bremen Grand Prix.

He has to understand the concept of activating the hind legs and letting go with the hand. The horse has to be activated without wanting to run off, without pulling on the hand. A trainer has to understand how to make a horse strong and powerful in the correct muscles, so the student and horse work in harmony. Power is used to enhance the beauty of the performance.

A trainer has to understand that when you apply an aid, you have to get an answer; you have to get a

Figure 1.3

"It lies in the hands of every single rider whether horse and rider feel relaxed. It must be every rider's supreme aim to create relaxation of mind and body." Klaus Balkenhol.

Mr. Balkenhol schools the horse Laredo in the piaffe. Note his relaxed and effective position. His heels are down, and the spurs do not touch the horse. The horse remains quiet and steady in the contact with a closed, foaming mouth. The rider's weight interacts with the horse's motion without interfering, because of the lack of tension. Mr. Balkenhol's shoulders and upper body remain soft as he teaches this horse one of the most difficult lessons in collection. Again, the muscles of the horse work, but are not tight like piano wires. Furthermore, Laredo shows significant topline development, the product of successful training. Mr. Balkenhol achieves this effect through the independence of his aids and by not driving while holding. "Using too much leg and hand at the same time is like driving a car with the brakes and gas applied simultaneously."

Figure 1.4

Klaus Balkenhol designed much of this facility. Note the rubber pavers on the covered aisle from the barn to the indoor so horses don't slip. Another nice feature is the concrete under the indoor kickboards so the arena drag doesn't damage the walls. This facilitates daily dragging and removal of the rut formed when horses are ridden along the track. These ruts can cause injuries to horses. The windows provide natural light, but the kickboards are high enough so horses can't see out; horses can be startled when things which are partially hidden by a low wall suddenly pop into view. Horses don't like surprises. A computer-controlled watering system keeps the arena dust-free for equines and humans. Daily exposure to large amounts of dust can cause horses (and people) to develop chronic coughs and worse. The water also helps to bind the footing, which is a mixture of sand and shavings.

---

reaction, but don't ask for too much and don't ask for things that a horse can't do. If you are not educating a horse properly, it leads to violence. Violence can be known and unknown. Mechanical riding can be violent because horses are broken instead of developed.

The theme of art is difficult. Forcing horses to piaffe on the spot, like you sometimes see today, is wrong; standing behind them and beating them with a whip until they lose all confidence. Soon they will no longer go down the centerline. The end result is a horse with no confidence or with soundness problems. Through correct training you teach horses to piaffe without going forward, by making the horse strong. Horses in earlier times were really worked. People knew how.

A trainer is one who can preserve and also improve the basic qualities of the gaits. That means that each gait stays pure, that the walk remains in a clear rhythm, that the trot does not become over-sensational, and

Figure 1.5

Klaus Balkenhol's barn allows each horse to see many other horses, promoting a herd feeling. The stalls in this barn form a ring around the "tack-island" behind the grooming area on the right. Good natural light and ventilation are provided through large windows on both sides of the barn. Additionally each stall is vented at the base. The stall grills are strong and high enough so horses cannot become entangled by kicking or striking through the bars, a type of injury more common than most believe. The barn features are designed for safety plus physical and mental comfort. Note the use of rubber pavers. Additionally, each horse is either turned out on a grass paddock or hand grazed at least once a day. "The horses need this to promote relaxation and happiness."

that the canter remains in three beats. These fundamentals are necessary in a Grand Prix horse. Unfortunately, today you see many Grand Prix horses that are not correct in their gaits. The canter has become four-beat, or it is tense. The trot may look great in front, but the hind legs are not active. The walk is lateral. Many times horses are ridden in an over-sensational way and they lose relaxation in their backs; the horse's back is very tense. These horses usually end up being seen more often in the vet clinic instead of the show arena.

What mental qualities are most important for a rider to develop in order to advance?

A competition rider should possess a moral maturity. He should be mature enough to be able to form an understanding, a working relationship with the creature,

Figure 1.6

Anabel Balkenhol rides Little Big Man, who is trotting nicely and using his topline. Horses learn by doing. Therefore, what the horse is doing is what he is learning. In other words, a rider who always fights with a horse and rides using only strong aids will teach this horse to be a strong fighter. A horse must trot correctly before a rider can develop correct muscles for the trot work. Of course, many mistakes happen along the way so only a patient, educated rider can successfully train a horse.

Figure 1.7

Balkenhol uses many hours of correct riding and many half halts to rebalance Little Big Man onto his haunches while keeping his back up and working. Note that the horse seeks proper contact with the bit.

Figure 1.8

Anabel Balkenhol plays the horse between the driving and restraining aids: a little leg to go forward, followed immediately by a little hand to slow down. In the half halts, the movement of her weight goes slightly against the motion of the horse. But she must be careful—too much against the motion and the horse will drop his back; too little and she will have little influence. All of the aids are used in harmony with the horse's gaits. This brings Little Big Man's weight back onto his haunches. Horses learn best when riders show them how to do things right rather than only correcting them for doing things wrong. Education builds confidence.

the horse. He should never treat his horse as a mechanical thing, or act like he has a contract with a machine. Instead, he should honor this animal and treat him as an equal partner. Out of this understanding come many great obligations for the rider, and the rider must be able to meet these obligations. He has to be able to maintain his horse in the required environment with all the little and big things attached. He has to make sure that his horse has good ground or good footing to travel upon, not ground that will cause the horse injury and pain. He has to make sure that his horse is shod properly, fed well, cared for, and so on, and so on.

What physical characteristics does a rider need?

A rider must be fit. He must keep himself fit. This means that a rider must do something besides riding to

Figure 1.9

"It is important for the horse's mind and body to let him gallop forward. Cantering forward and galloping develop a horse's hindquarters and build muscles that are needed for piaffe and passage. It is also good for the horse's mental relaxation and happiness." Klaus Balkenhol.

stay fit. He must gymnastically develop his muscles, and he must do exercises to remain supple. He must maintain agility. He must train and exercise, which also helps him to understand this process. All of these things are necessary for a rider who wants to ride competitively before he even makes contact with a horse.

How would you define a successful day of training?

It is important that a training program shows progress. But sometimes this progress is slow; you can't get results from one day to the next. Sometimes it takes weeks or even months until the student and the horse begin to understand a lesson[1] and perform as a team. It is important in the training to always start with easy exercises and also to end with easy exercises that the rider and horse understand. This helps build confidence in both horse and rider. In this way the trainer can develop a program that builds every day on what was learned before. This is very important.

---

[1] The German term of *lesson* is better than the term *movement* which is most common in the USA. If a rider teaches a horse a lesson well, the horse learns what is expected of him and becomes a partner with the rider. This helps the understanding of self-carriage. The word *movement* implies mechanics. As Klaus Balkenhol stated, "Mechanical riding can be violent because horses are broken instead of developed." Think of riding a half pass or a shoulder-in as a *lesson*, not as a *movement*.

Figure 1.10

Klaus Balkenhol instructs a student about addressing a common problem: difficulty bending to one side, in this case the left. Mr. Balkenhol said, "It is important apply the aids correctly so the horse uses the proper muscles. Next, the rider must allow sufficient time for these muscles to develop. Resorting to draw reins in these circumstances will not correct the problem. The horse's training can progress only after the contact becomes more even." Mr. Balkenhol instructs the student to use the left half pass to help the horse with bending. They work on increasing the engagement, which creates an uphill horse and helps lighten the forehand and the contact—especially the contact on the left rein. The half pass helps keep the horse's right hind leg stepping under his center of gravity while the horse bends to the left. The rider should apply an aid only as needed to make a change. The sideways driving leg should relax as soon as the horse responds sideways. This allows self-carriage in the lateral work. The most important part of giving an aid is the release of the aid.

Figure 1.11
The house and the barn at the Balkenhols' form an equilateral "L," two legs of one continuous building. The structure frames two sides of the garden, thus providing equal views to equines and humans.

Figure 1.12
The Balkenhols' house from the front.

When is a horse ready to advance?

A horse is ready to learn more when he is strong enough in his current lessons. This means that the horse is muscularly developed and carries the rider with ease and confidence. Also the horse must understand what the rider wants and expects from him. This is very important. The horse must learn the leg aids, rein aids, and the weight[2] aids. When a horse has reached this level of development, he is ready to learn lessons (schools).

---

[2] In Germany one often hears the term "*weight aid*" instead of "*seat aid*," which is common in the USA. The influence of the seat is determined by the rider's position and the way that his mass interacts with the horse's motion.

Figure 1.13
A computer-controlled watering system prevents dust in the indoor. When activated, the sprinkler travels along the ceiling-track in the middle of the indoor. The system can be programmed to water drier regions a little more and shady, wetter areas a little less.

Figure 1.14
The control center for the indoor's watering system.

When has a horse reached its limit?

Well, a horse lives through his memories. First, a horse performs a task. Next he repeats this task until he has learned it. Through this process the horse eventually knows what he is supposed to do when the rider or trainer applies very specific aids. We have a very specific palette of lessons for the horse to learn. However, when a horse reaches an old age, we have to be careful. Horses are capable of learning new things even at a very old age, but sometimes the horse no longer has the strength to perform the task well. For example, the piaffe requires a great deal of strength to perform properly. We should not expect an older horse to learn to do this well. Eventually we reach a point where we cannot—or should not—ask for more from the horse.

Have you seen trainers who have brought a horse to Intermediate 1, and then they try to train this horse to Grand Prix? After several months, the horse is not doing well at Grand Prix, but he also can no longer perform well at Prix St. Georges.

OK, I have seen this also: A rider who can't bring his horse to Grand Prix because he is not able to do so. However, nearly every horse can learn all of the lessons in Grand Prix. Some will perform the lessons better than others. Some will be more beautiful than others. But if you have a rider or trainer who can't train beyond Prix St. Georges and this rider works with a horse until the horse has reached an old age, it will be very difficult to train this horse to Grand Prix. Another example would be a rider who trains a lot of counter canter. If a horse does counter canter as a six-, seven-, eight-, and even nine-year-old, it will be very difficult to teach this horse flying changes. This becomes a difficult situation. This is when horses bump into barriers that stop them from progressing, but these barriers are created by the riders.

Figure 1.15
Young four-year-old stallions display their talent at the German Championships for Young Horses. These shows for young horses are immensely popular in Germany—tens of thousands attend. There are divisions for dressage horses, jumpers, and three-day event horses. Most arenas have standing room only (to see anything you have to be either tall or early). In Germany, the young horse championships are more popular than nearly all Grand Prixs.

In this situation, with the flying changes, it is important to monitor whether the horse understands what is being asked of him, that the aids for the changes are clear and accurate. This situation presents many problems. However, one should not resort to violence. Violence will not get the rider anywhere. The rider must use his knowledge of exercises to teach the horse. For example, he can cause the horse to lose his balance in the canter, and in this moment of unbalance, he shows the horse how to canter in the new canter lead.

It will be easiest for this horse to learn changes with another rider, not with the rider that introduced life to the horse without flying changes and only rode the counter canter. However, sometimes the horse and rider can change and learn together in this situation. Flying changes are one of the most natural lessons for the horse.

This example also applies to other lessons in dressage. The trainer must think of exercises to get the horse to "rethink" the way he has learned a task.

When does a rider need a new horse?

If a rider wants to compete, it is somewhat different than for a *free-time rider* (pleasure rider). A pleasure rider can own and ride the same horse for a very long period of time. But this rider is also responsible for caring for this horse when the horse is no longer able to be ridden. The responsibility of a rider is very, very great, to take care of his horse. It's not enough for the rider to care for the horse only when he can sit on it; instead the responsibility grows when the horse becomes dependent on special care. Every rider must know that at this point he has problems that are sometimes more difficult to solve than the problems encountered when he could ride his horse. He must make sure that the horse is properly cared for, or if the horse is no longer able to live comfortably, judged by what is in the best interest of the horse, he must accompany the horse to be put down. First when these things are solved, he can begin to decide if he needs a new horse. There is an ethic

Figure 1.16
Anabel Balkenhol takes Little Big Man on a walk after his work. It is important for horses to get out of the arena. They should go on walks and trail rides to promote mental happiness.

that says that these situations must be taken care of by the rider. Only after these problems are resolved should the rider think about getting a new horse.

For the competition rider, the situation is a little different. As the horse gets older, he may decide to give the horse to somebody who can ride the horse a little and care for the horse, a situation where the horse can be ridden on the trails and exercised a little. But a competition rider needs to have some *nachwuchs Pferde* (up-and-coming young horses) that he is developing. He can't wait until his horse is fifteen or sixteen years old and can't compete anymore. At this point he can't all of the sudden decide that he needs a new horse. An international rider needs to have several horses that he is developing, so that when one isn't working out competitively he has another coming along. But very few riders manage to do this. A competition rider needs a new horse when the shows tell him that it is necessary.

How would you define a great horse?

One that matures beyond all of the things that he would normally detest. In a customary or normal sense, if you have a horse that has a normal trot, but this horse learns to constantly display a fantastic *losgelassenheit*,³ I find this great, for me personally. When a horse has a great passage or piaffe, for example Gracioso or Farbenfroh (twice the World Champion under Nadine Capellmann-Biffar), horses that I recently trained to do these lessons; these horses displayed great talent for passage and piaffe, like almost no other horses. This designates greatness.

Did you have a favorite horse? If so, which one was it and what was he like?

If I had to pick a favorite, it was Goldstern. I have to say that because I knew him from a very young age. We grew up together. But I have always been very practical around horses, and I love all horses, each in its own way. I have to thank Goldstern in particular because he made everything possible. But then I must also thank the people around Goldstern, like the police department that allowed me to do duty at the horse competitions.

And how was Goldstern to be around—daily riding, in the stall, or at a show?

Goldstern was a relatively difficult horse. He wasn't so easy to handle and his body wasn't what you would look at and say, "Wow! That is a nice dressage horse." He had relatively short legs. Concerning his head, he was always very interested in everything around him. He could be stubborn. He could say, "I want to do *this*.

---

³ It is preferable to translate this term as loose-letting-ness or loose-allowing-ness. The horse allows supple looseness through his entire body and into his movement. This happens after a horse has achieved serenity or tranquility. The horse and the rider are relaxed and loose together.

In English we say you can make a horse supple. In German you develop *losgelassenheit*; you cannot force it. You cannot make it happen. If you ride well, the horse allows himself to relax and become supple.

Losgelassenheit is exemplified by a swinging back and lowered neck which allows the horse to travel in an even rhythm and seek quiet, proper contact with a closed, lightly chewing and foaming mouth.

Figure 1.17
One of the many vendor aisles at the German Championships for Young Horses.

If you want me to do *that*, I don't want to, it's the last thing that I want to do." He was quite frightened at times around things that were unfamiliar to him and wouldn't want to cooperate. These were all things that made my life difficult.

But he had an unbelievable will to work. He was motivated in the tenth degree. He had very good endurance and a lot of power and an iron will to do something. He wanted to go, to move. He was never a horse that couldn't be worked through his difficulties.

How would you define excellence?

When something that is normally difficult becomes simple, that is excellence. Or if you do something and

Figure 1.18

Anabel Balkenhol properly executes a corner on her mount Flashback. The corner is one of the simplest and most incorrectly ridden exercises. Note that she has bent her horse without having the hind legs drift into the corner; he tracks straight. She controls the horse's bend using both of her legs as needed. The inside leg bends and the outside leg keeps the haunches from swinging out. Note the steady contact. She will ride deeper into the corner as the horse warms up. As the degree of collection increases, riders should ride deeper into the corners.

you have a very positive result, that is excellence. These can be very small things. Small things after a period of time can become very large things. That is excellence.

If you could change one thing about the world of competitive dressage, what would it be? What is the biggest disadvantage of competitive dressage?

I would want to change people's perceptions about the education of young horses, that we would again give them time to develop an education. I would like to introduce exercises that develop riding as an art throughout the levels and into the highest classes.

The other would be to educate the judges on well-ridden horses, if this were possible, of course—so judges could learn to feel what it is like to ride on well-schooled horses, gymnastically developed horses that were educated according to classical principles. The judges could develop a feeling that could later help to educate their eyes. Then they could look at a horse and say, "That one might feel a

Figure 1.19

Klaus Balkenhol schools Stefan Wolf riding the five-year-old stallion His Highness at the German Championships.

little like this, or perhaps a little like that, but that one doesn't feel right, even though the horse is presented very well in a mechanical way in the competition arena."

Many times the piaffe is ridden too forward. The horses push their way forward and don't pick their feet up as diagonal pairs. The judges should learn what it feels like when a horse piaffes *on the spot*. This is a good piaffe. If a horse goes forward, it is not as good of a piaffe, even if forward steps are allowed. This example applies to other lessons as well.

What is the best thing about competitive dressage? Are there good influences from showing?

I believe that competition riding has to be founded upon the health and happiness of the horse. This is very important. If we establish that as the first condition, then the sport of horses can offer a lot to people, because it develops a relationship between horses and animals. [Klaus Balkenhol caught his error and chuckled.] Of course, I mean between horses and people, not between horses and animals. Competitive riding requires a

Figure 1.20

Anabel Balkenhol rides Preston, who takes a long look at the camera.

relationship between horses and people. In our time we are experiencing a technicalization of our lives from the machines that we have built. In this respect, it is good that we have horses in sport. But, what I meant earlier about young horses in sport is that commerce is playing too big a role at the shows—business.

People start to expect young horses to look great. If somebody is looking for a young horses they want it to look very developed, even though physically and mentally the horse is not fit or ready to be so developed. In other words, people have to learn to be patient.

In earlier times people who wanted to be officers in the armed forces, in any branch, were required to complete a tour of duty in the horse stable for one year. They had to learn to get along with horses by having duty with the cavalry. This required them to learn subordination. This was very important at that time for the officers in Germany. It meant that these men had to learn to serve the needs of the horse. They had to learn to step back in certain situations. They learned that anger and violence don't work, that they must somehow build a trusting relationship with these powerful animals; they all saw this eventually. These lessons helped to develop the character of the person. They had a positive influence on the person.

Therefore, it is a good thing that we have horses today, and that we have horses in sport. People learn because of this other consciousness that they can't influence with violence. A rider must first achieve the goal of a good relationship with the horse, and then he must acquire a proper education in order to progress and train any lessons. This is necessary if the rider wants to succeed.

I just thought of something that Reiner Klimke said about competitions. At home many horses are world champions. But under the conditions of competition, you really see how good the horse is mentally, and the correct rideability. This may have nothing to do with how the judges score the test. Instead, the rider gets a good idea of how the training is going, especially if he watches a video later. A rider at home will not always ask for what the exercises and movements demand, because that can be difficult. But when you are at a show, then you must perform the movements. It doesn't matter which movement it is, but the rider has a test to ride. Often the rider finds that things go differently than when he goes through the motions at home. At home he can have a positive result and then at the show he has a negative result.

At the show, the rider sees if things worked out like he thought they would. He notices that, ah-ha, I have a problem here. At home, I thought that this worked well, but here, where a lot of people are watching, things didn't go as well as they do at home. Maybe the horse got tense, but the rider learns where he must practice more. So on a personal level a rider can get a lot from showing.

I would also like to add, that there was a time when I had to get the horse ready myself at the shows, when I drove the horse to the show and cared for him. I was responsible to make sure that he was bedded down properly at night. He was in my care twenty-four hours a day. When I think back to this now, I realize that this was an unbelievably important exercise. And also to get ready for the test, that one knows the smallest rules, and how the horse acts in these new surroundings. It was important to see how the horse reacted and to take the time to think through things. This helps to understand the nature of the horse. When a rider rides at a show, he should spend time with the horse and get to know him in this new environment. And not do like many jumping riders, who send the horses with the grooms. They show up at the arena with polished boots. The horse is ready and waiting. They ride and then leave the horse with the groom. The rider has spent a total of thirty minutes with the horse.

I think it is important for the rider to build a connection with the horse, by spending time, around the clock; I mean that when the horse sleeps, the rider sleeps also. But through spending time together, the rider and horse become closer. This is very important. This develops a person. It builds him. And at the show these conditions develop a rider more. He matures more.

Unfortunately, I've noticed many dressage riders today let everything be done for them. They have little contact with the horse.

When I think about Nadine [Nadine Capellmann-Biffar, Olympic team gold medalist, Olympic individual bronze medalist, and twice the WEG individual gold medalist], she drives her horses to the show and unloads them herself. She is very involved with their care and watches over them continuously. I mean she sleeps in the hotel at night, but she is crazy enough that she would sleep at the barn if she thought she had to. These qualities make the true horse-person, Nadine Capellmann. She is there not just for the success; this is not a case of a blind ego. She is always thinking, "Are my horses well?"

Many riders don't have these qualities. They only see the commercial side of dressage, the business. My horse wins, and from this victory, I can support my stable and do other things. But Nadine, I have to say, is a horse-person of the first order. She flew with her horse to Sydney. She wanted to be with him for the long trip.

What was your greatest setback? Many people might believe that Klaus Balkenhol has had an easy life. He won this and that. He was a champion. He never had a tough life.

Yes, I have had a lot of good luck in my life, I have to admit. I had a lot to do with horses in my youth. I was both required to work with horses and also allowed to work with horses. As a young man I went to police training. At the time I didn't know about the riding opportunities that would be available to me; I knew that riding was a possibility in police training, but I didn't join for that reason. That came later. Then I met my wife. We shared a love of horses, and together we deepened our love of horses. We also wanted to explore the knowledge of horsemanship. That means that we wanted to get to know horses better, so we bought books, went to shows, and watched. We watched in the warm-up arenas to see how people interacted with their horses. We have experienced many beautiful things together, but we also have experienced some things that were not so nice. And so a simple conclusion [about my championship life] does not exist. I rode my first Grand Prix at age thirty-nine. Others had already won at the Olympics when they were twenty-one. Whether you speak of Isabel Werth, Nicole Uphoff, or Monica Theodorescu, they had ridden at a relatively young age in the Olympics. I was lucky that I received special help from the police department which allowed me to compete while on duty with my police horse, so I continued to draw my policeman's salary. However, I didn't receive a lot of outside financial help with my riding until I was already showing internationally, then the *Deutsche Sport Hilfe* (this translates as German Sport Help, which is a German corporation that provides financial aid to athletes) gave me lots of help. Judith and I had to make a lot of arrangements and plans in order to reach the international levels. At the same time we had a family. We had a daughter who had to also suffer a little under these conditions. She had to make sacrifices because of the family's involvement with the horses. She came up a little short at times. I think about this sometimes.

What were your setbacks?

If I am going to talk about setbacks, then I have to say that one of the greatest is when we had to say goodbye to the horses that made the success possible in this sport. First Rabauke died here on this farm. This was very painful. There have been other horses also that were not known internationally that we have lost. Then there was Goldstern, of course; this was a horror for me because he just wasn't so old and he had always been so healthy. There were never problems with him. But, one day he got colic and there weren't any choices; he couldn't be saved. This was a tragedy because this horse is the one that showed me the way. Both of these horses, being police horses, were unique in the sport of dressage and in the history of dressage. They were bought for 4,000DM and 6,000DM (roughly $2,000 and $3,000). Nobody thought that these horses would compete internationally. This made it more difficult for me to say goodbye.

Of course, other setbacks were when I have lost friends and relatives and when I lost my parents.

Figure 1.21

Klaus Balkenhol's posture and carriage exude confidence and understanding. He rides and trains like an ad for classical dressage, an example of what dressage should be. Violence has no part in his art with horses. He motivates the horses with careful teaching; he trains the desired responses to each aid. He also takes time to make each horse loose and supple. This is accomplished in great part by correctly riding half halts. Most of the time Klaus Balkenhol's half halts are only visible by their effect on the horse. He creates a momentary shortening of the stride, followed by an increase in animation. "First you shorten the strides, and only if the horse is good in the hand does the rider ask the horse to work more through careful application of the driving aids. If the horse is pulling in the half halt and the rider drives forward, then the horse gets driven onto the forehand."

These things are a part of life that one must go through. And to see something positive in all of this, one has to dedicate himself to building something new and better for those that follow and the horses that I now work with. I think it is very necessary that a person has simply experienced these things. But very hard setbacks, thank God, I have not yet experienced.

What was your greatest victory?

Concerning horses, it was the Olympics in Barcelona, and the World Championships in The Haag, which was the test for horses in international competition. Then I would have to include my win at the German Championships in Muenster against very stiff competition. That really helped us to advance in the sport of dressage. It gave me a lot of exposure and motivation.

What was your worst ride?

My worst ride was at Lipiza during the European Championships. I was in first place, about to enter the freestyle, and I was the favorite to win. While waiting for the rider before me to finish, I heard a thunderstorm rapidly approaching. I remember Harry Boldt saying, "You better go in now." But I couldn't. I had to wait for the rider to finish.

As I entered the stadium, the storm struck. Wind and rain howled. Trash flew through the air. Hundreds of people raised their umbrellas and ran for cover. On top of that, a cushion blew against Goldstern's leg, and he became entangled momentarily in the straps. He kicked himself free. Primitive survival instincts threatened to overwhelm him. This was too much for any horse. Although I knew that all of his instincts were telling him to flee, he stayed there with me. He was a hero.

At that moment, the bell rang. It was time to ride my test. I did my best to calm Goldstern, to tune him into the subtleties of dressage, but he was too frightened. The sudden onslaught of wind and rain showed no signs of abating. He did his best. Under these circumstances, he was my champion. But needless to say, we dropped from first place.

This was bad luck, but in general, any test where I make mistakes is the hardest for me, the hardest to dismiss. Mistakes that a horse makes aren't so bad, not so bad at all. But when a horse doesn't do so well because of my errors, I have a hard time sleeping at night. It hurts me very much. But, I have to add to this, that I find something worthwhile in every test that I ride. There is always something positive in it . . . to learn for the next time. If you don't make any mistakes, you can't learn anything for the next time. Everyone must make mistakes—not intentionally, of course—but when I make a mistake, I remember it and which situation caused the error. I perform better the next time. Then, these mistakes aren't so bad.

What was your most memorable ride?

It was in the World Championships at The Haag, in the Kür. This ride was very well received by a large audience, including the Americans who were also there. Goldstern performed his best. After the show, many people told me that I should have won, but the judges saw things differently. One of the most difficult aspects of competitive dressage is the judging; sometimes it is disappointing even though the judges try their best. As competitors, we must always be happy when our mounts perform their best.

Do you have advice for a striving rider?

I give clinics for the Piaffe Foerder Prize. This is a program that many professionals participate in, and it centers on a test in which riders can participate until they are twenty-five years old. This means that the young riders who finish their Young Riders program at age twenty-one don't fall into a hole; they aren't required to compete against all of the seniors in an open division of Grand Prix. They ride in an easier Grand Prix where they can learn and develop until they are ready for the open division. I give clinics for this program two times a year, and I have students that ride these tests. One of them is Carola Koppelmann, who did very well. She won most of her tests and was then able to make the jump to the big Grand Prix. She is now in the "B Cadre" of riders—in other words, long listed. This was a good example of how a young rider gets support, then is able to advance to international competition.

Why is dressage important in the twenty-first century?

I believe that dressage and horses in general belong in the lives of people. Horses are not house pets, and they are also not cows, deer, pigs, or sheep, which

Figure 1.22

Princess Natalie zu Sayn-Wittgenstein training piaffe on her Danish gelding, Digby. Once again, Klaus Balkenhol instructed the rider to use the half halt properly, to separate the driving and restraining aids and yet use them in harmony with the horse. "Your horse must first learn to respond to light aids and to accept the response to a light aid. This is very important. He has to know what the leg means and also what the hand means. He is not allowed to run through your hand." This degree of independence of the aids is only possible with a rider who sits relaxed in the saddle. Too much tension in the rider will interfere with the horse's motion. "You must play the horse back onto the spot in the piaffe. A rider must not clamp with the aids."

must exist as commodities to support people; although there are breeds of horses that are raised, marketed, and slaughtered for these reasons.

But in general, I am of the opinion that horses and the sport horse as a companion to people, a comrade, belong with people in the twenty-first century and also in the twenty-second century. Horses show people that there are other wills and other consciences.

If you apply this question to dressage horses, then I think that the close contact with the horse helps lead a person through life. Individuals get to experience interaction with an animal, a conciseness that doesn't allow itself to have just anything done to it,

Figure 1.23

At Klaus Balkenhol's, Pierre St. Jacques receives training with his horse Lucky Tiger. This pair helped the USA win the team gold medal at the 2003 Pan Am Games. They train here to make the big jump from the small to the big tour. Note the steady contact and the relaxed, yet working, muscles of the horse and rider, a Balkenhol trademark.

like a rabbit or something similar. People around horses have to think about how they can get into the horse's head and win this mass of muscle over to their side.

I would like to add that horse sports in general have changed a lot over the last fifty to sixty years. Let's say over the last sixty years. The horse was a working animal at that time. The horse was used for agriculture or in the army to transport people. Some horses pulled cannons and all kinds of things. Then came the technicalization starting around fifty years ago, and horses were used less for work. People had to think, "Well, we have so many horses. What are we going to do with all of them?" They started to ride for a hobby and began horse sports. Then they developed the breeding programs and bred sport horses. There has always been an upward curve to this. They continue to breed better and better horses for what we need in horse sports.

Then the business of sport horses started. More and more people fished in this pool and made money breeding horses, good horses. The farmers who bred these horses wanted to make money very early. Consequently, these young horses had to look like they could do everything at a very early age. And this made a lot of horses kaput. They couldn't take the pressure, so many were broken—both physically and mentally.

But visiting horse shows, or holding shows where everybody can see horses in sport—this openness in working with horses has the advantage of introducing youth to horses. They can be little baby-shows on a farm, it doesn't matter. These shows ensure that horses don't get lost or forgotten in our technical world. This is why it is very important that we have shows. Then everybody knows that there are animals in this world that people made useful for humanity. And the act of preserving this work with animals falls into the hands of those with experience. Then we come full circle again, to the point that I believe it is very important that we have open events and shows with horses, open to the public. It doesn't matter if they are cross-country, jumping, or dressage, just that they involve horses.

I think it is also important that we keep horse sports in the Olympics. We then present this concept in all openness to the world. It doesn't matter if the people watching are in China or who knows where, just that they see that mankind and animals belong together, that we both belong to nature.

This has been about horses, but there are other animals that mankind has worked together with, elephants in India or wherever they are; this is very important. With camels, people also make sports. When people no longer need these animals in a technical world, they can use them in sports. Working elephants . . . they are not used so much anymore. Except in the bush, they have to use them.

But here in Germany, they have discovered a new job for working horses. They are used for logging. They do much less damage to the forest floor than the machines; these wide tires from the tractors, they compress the soil so no water gets through and they make big ruts. Then the trees no longer grow.

The horses are better at this. This was newly discovered again . . . a new and old discovery. And so, I am of the opinion that horse-people must do everything possible to bring a system of people working together with horses, in a manner that is based on the humane treatment of these animals, out into the open where everybody can see and appreciate this. Of course, this means keeping horse sports in the Olympics. This is very important. I believe also that this will be so.

Is there anything else that you would like to share with the dressage world?

When I ride, I first like to place myself somewhere. "Placing myself" means that somehow with this living being I can build a unity, as good a one as possible. That's what I think of, that I get into the movement of the horse, but that I do not disturb the apparatus of movement; instead, I, through my aids, give wings to the horse to move in a more beautiful way. The horse has to learn to move from the rider, from the work and influence of the rider. The horse has to learn to go with the rider in such a way that he moves just as nice as he would move if he were in the wild and without a rider. The horse has to build muscles so he can hold himself in a very certain way, while moving, whether he is walking, trotting, or cantering.

I think this art is necessary for people in these times.

Figure 1.24

A group of riders works in Klaus Balkenhol's outdoor arena, including USA team rider Pierre St. Jacques. "It is important for the riders to have time to work on their own, to think about things and try things while I watch." This is true at all levels of riding at many barns in Germany. There are very few private lessons, although riders get individual attention as needed. Riders learn to work under constant supervision, but there is also plenty of time to experiment in between instructions. In contrast to this, many lessons in the USA are private and riders receive constant feedback, but this allows little time for riders to work things out on their own. Dressage is an art defined inside of strict parameters. However, within the accepted guidelines, all students must learn to develop their own version of art that suits their body. This can be difficult under the constant verbal barrage of a daily private lesson. For those that do not have daily training, another problem lurks on the horizon. Things can proceed farther down the wrong path before a correction is received.

Figure 1.25

The riders begin the work session with a long period of walk on a loose rein. "This is to let the horses' muscles begin to warm up," Klaus Balkenhol says. "It is important for riders not to take the reins too soon. The neck and back need to loosen first before the rider begins work. Riders also need to take many walk breaks throughout the training session to help keep the horse relaxed."

Figure 1.26

At the German Championships, Stefan Wolf allows the five-year-old stallion His Highness to chew the reins out of his hands in the sitting trot. The stallion stretches down and forward with his nose, but the contact remains true. A horse should not snatch the reins from the rider's hands. The horse should slowly and quietly stretch down as the rider lets the reins slide between his fingers. The frame[4] of the horse is long, but the horse continues to work through his back and seeks contact.

The rider must exercise great care in keeping the horse's back supple, relaxed, and working properly. The horse's back not only bridges the horse's hindquarters to his forehand, made disparate by the weight of the rider; the back bridges communication between two species. The horse's back is an integral part of the "apparatus of movement." Klaus Balkenhol also says, "Control the horse using correct aids and you get his back." The horse's back begins to swing and relax. "Get their backs and you win their minds." Dressage becomes a language of motion.

---

[4] "Frame" in German also means attitude. In English we say that you can see a person's attitude by the way that he carries himself, or we sometimes refer to a *frame of mind*. A good rider will not force a horse into a frame; he will shape the attitude of a horse as he changes its outline.

[5] This test for five-year-old horses is "L" level, which is equivalent in the amount of engagement required to do a second level test in the USA. However, an important distinction is that the German test and the FEI "L" tests do not have lateral movements, i.e., no shoulder-in or haunches in. As Klaus Balkenhol says, "After a horse understands and accepts collection, then lessons such as shoulder-in are very easy for the horse."

Figure 1.27

His Highness shows good suspension in the medium canter,[5] a product of strong and supple back muscles.

Training Questions

YOUNG HORSE

At what age should a horse be backed?

Generally at age three. Naturally at this age we do not work the horses too hard. They are made familiar with life as a dressage horse. We work on gaining their confidence and trust. We start to build the muscles that they will need to carry a rider.

What mistakes do you often observe in the training of young horses?

Often young horses are pushed too hard. They are expected to look like trained horses at a very young age. This causes a lot of damage to these horses. Often, they have soundness problems. People don't take the time to develop the correct muscles. If they are having a problem, they put draw-reins on the horse without thinking twice. Instead of taking time to train and develop the correct muscles, people force the horse into compliance. The horses are not worked properly.

Young horses are often ridden in an over-sensational way, and the judges reward this. In many cases, the basics of the training scale are ignored, such as rhythm, suppleness, and impulsion. Young horses are often tense because they are pushed too hard for bigger movement and bigger gaits. Recently the judges at the World Championships for Young Horses awarded a 9.8 to a horse for a trot with rhythm faults. They said they would have scored the horse higher but that he showed slight irregularities behind.

What should a three-year-old horse know at the end of the first year of training?

The horse should have developed *losgelassenheit* under the rider. The horse learns *losgelassenheit* through understanding and achieving a better balance under the rider. The horse should have an understanding of part of the scale of training, namely rhythm, suppleness, and contact. When the horse understands contact, the rider can begin to maintain impulsion and start to straighten the horse. The basic and natural gaits of the horse must remain pure. No faults should be caused by the rider in the natural rhythm of the walk, trot, and canter.

The horse should understand half halts. He should allow himself to be slowed down and to be ridden forward. He should be able to travel slightly sideways in lateral work without too much collection.

I believe that all horses should learn these things without becoming specialized. These concepts remain the same for jumpers, three-day-event horses, and dressage horses. This is basic education for all horses.

When do you begin to train lateral movements?

You can begin to train leg-yielding early, but only if it doesn't interfere with the basic gaits of the horse. The horse's natural rhythm in the walk, trot, and canter must remain pure. This is very important. Only if these conditions are met can the rider train leg-yielding. Horses are not ready to learn shoulder-in or half pass in their first year under saddle, so leg-yielding is a good exercise. The horse becomes used to moving sideways from one leg. He becomes accustomed to the leg aids and to unilateral aids. The horse should have a good understanding of leg-yielding after the first year of training.

Where or in which parts of the arena do you train leg-yielding?

I always begin to train leg-yielding on the long side. I flex the horse's head to the outside of the arena.[6] In this way I use the rail or kickboard. I then push the horse's haunches toward the inside track. The horse learns to find his balance while he moves sideways. Through finding his balance as he moves sideways, he learns to engage. This is the most effective way to teach leg-yielding.

At what age do you begin to show horses?

I believe that a young three-year-old should have a quiet and relaxing first year under saddle. If a rider takes such a young horse to a show, he will train longer and harder. This is automatic, and this should not happen. The rider should do normal work and train through the winter. He can then show the horse as a four-year-old in the spring in material[7] classes. A rider who works a young horse too hard will cause damage and lameness problems. This should not happen.

---

[6] Proper flexing aids are important. The rider must be careful to play with his fingers and be ready to ride forward so he doesn't upset the rhythm. As the horse changes flexion, the rein on the outside of the arena becomes the inside rein by definition. When a horse flexes properly only the axis joint is involved; the rest of the spine stays straight.

[7] Dressage suitability is the term used most often in the USA for material classes. In these classes the horses do not perform a test. Instead several horses walk, trot, and canter together in the arena at the same time.

Figure 1.28
Seven-year-old gelding. Won and placed at small tour. Trained by Klaus Balkenhol.

Figure 1.29
Four-year-old stallion. He came to Klaus Balkenhol with training problems several months prior to this photo.

Figure 1.30
Eight-year-old gelding. Schooling many Grand Prix lessons. Trained by Klaus Balkenhol.

Figure 1.31
Ten-year-old mare. Trained by Dr. Schulten-Baumer. One of the top Grand Prix horses in Germany.

Figures 1.28–1.35

Compare the topline muscles in the top four pictures of horses trained by dressage masters with the four photos on the next page, which were taken at the FEI World Championship for Young Horses. The horses competing in the World Championship show little topline development. Although the ages differ in the two groups of horses, the four-year-old in fig. 1.29 has already developed a topline that will serve him well as he advances to the upper levels.

Of course, any horse can be caught at a bad moment by a photograph. However, the pictures of these horses were consistent with many others shot at the same time. Another differing factor is that the top four pictures were taken while schooling and the following four were taken in competition, so tension is a factor; these pictures shouldn't be used as too much of a critique of the next four horses. Additionally, the neck is a small part of the over-all training picture. However, the pictures still make an interesting point. And too much tension or a bad picture cannot make a muscle vanish.

Figure 1.32
Five-year-old stallion. FEI World Championship for five-year-olds.

Figure 1.33
Six-year-old stallion. FEI World Championship for six-year-olds.

Figure 1.34
Five-year-old stallion. FEI World Championship for five-year-olds.

Figure 1.35
Six-year-old stallion. FEI World Championships for six-year-olds. Some good muscle development.

Figure 1.36
His Highness, at Klaus Balkenhol's arena, demonstrates the footfall of the canter as described in classical dressage.

Figure 1.37
A moment of suspension is followed by the striking of the outside hind leg, followed by the diagonal pair (outside front–inside hind).

Figure 1.38
Finally, the inside front hits the ground.

Figure 1.39

2004 and 2005 World Champion Florencio 2 as he starts his spectacular extended canter. Already a dissociation of the diagonal pair is evident. The inside hind will land before the outside front. Florencio 2 lowers his croup so deeply as he brings his hind legs under that his inside hind strikes well before his outside front.

Figure 1.40

This picture demonstrates a clear dissociation of the diagonal pair of legs in the canter. This differs from a traditional four-beat canter where the outside front hits before the inside hind, giving the canter a disjointed and heavy look. Florencio 2 seems to fly. Equine biomechanic experts such as Dr. Hillary Clayton and Dr. Holmström have documented that judges place horses higher which show this type of dissociation of a diagonal pair of legs, the hind foot landing before the front foot. This remains consistent from beginning levels to Grand Prix.

Figure 1.41

Notice also that Florencio 2's outside hind lifts from the ground well before the inside front strikes the ground. This is consistent with other horses that are capable of extending their strides to a great extent. Two panels of judges at two consecutive World Championships rewarded this canter with a 10. The judges have decided that this canter is ideal.

Figure 1.42

Six-year-old World Champion French Kiss demonstrates a traditional footfall in the extended canter.

Figure 1.43

French Kiss received an 8.80 on his canter.

Figure 1.44

Note that in comparison to Florencio 2 (Fig. 1.41), French Kiss's right hind remains on the ground even though the height of the left front in both pictures is approximately the same.

Figure 1.45
This horse in the counter canter shows the type of dissociation that is normally considered a four-beat canter.

Figure 1.46
Notice that the outside front leg (left front) strikes the ground before the inside hind, giving the horse a somewhat lateral gait. The left hooves hit the ground first, followed by the right hooves.

Figure 1.47
Perhaps this horse was caught in a bad moment. From a very talented horse you can have a bad picture, and from an untalented horse you can take a great picture. He received an 8 on this canter.

COLLECTION

When do you begin to train collection?

Young horses can learn about collection. The rein back teaches collection. The horse moves more weight onto his haunches and steps back with diagonal pairs of legs. A horse must collect when he reins back, otherwise he cannot do this exercise properly, so collection begins here. However, if a young horse offers collection, let's say he gets excited and does half steps or even piaffe or passage, then the rider should reward this horse and show him that he has done something desirable. But the rider should not encourage and ask a very young horse to piaffe or passage. That would be wrong. A four-year-old can do a little collected canter if he is developed enough. He should be able to shorten his strides in the trot also while maintaining energy. He should understand the half halt without the rider having to pull on the mouth. He should understand shortening from the riders *kreutz*[8] and legs. It is very important in these early stages of collection that the rider does not pull too much on the horse's mouth and that the rider rides from back to front. The horse should learn to understand collection and be schooled in collection through the proper use of aids by the rider.

Do you use one form of lateral work more often than the others?

I always think of young horses when answering questions such as these. I believe that a young horse must first be able to understand and accept the half halts, and then he can begin to understand collection.

---

[8] *Kreutz* translated means cross and also refers to the lumbar region in a person, roughly the area where a person's belt crosses his spine. Dancers, martial artists, and gymnasts refer to this area as their center, and it plays an important part in developing their physical and mental balance. Riding half halts from the *kreutz*, or lower back, is a term that is used more often in Germany than riding half halts from the seat. Again, this concept reinforces the idea of an interaction between the rider's balanced weight and the horse's motion.

Some horses learn this very fast and some might take a year. After a horse understands and accepts collection, then lessons such as shoulder-in are very easy for the horse. But riders should never force horses to do these exercises. They should not ride with violence. This would be a big step backwards in the education of the horse. Riders should use their aids in such a way that they teach the horse to understand the lesson. Shoulder-in and also half pass can be taught easily to a horse that understands how to carry weight on his haunches and travel in good balance with a rider.

Which combinations of lateral work do you prefer?

The young horse first learns to accept the unilateral aids by leg-yielding. Next it is natural that a horse learns a small amount of shoulder-in or shoulder-fore. This means that the horse is not bent too much in the lateral movement; that comes later. In the leg-yield, the horse was taught to travel sideways with a straight spine with a small amount of positioning or flexion at the poll. Therefore, we introduce the shoulder-in slowly, with a small amount of bend. Riding shoulder-in is the best preparation for the other lateral lessons.

Later, it is important that a rider keeps in mind the footfall or system of movement in the trot when he begins to train half pass. If we take a left shoulder-in, for example, then the inside legs of the horse are crossing in front of the outside legs just as they would in a half pass to the right. Of course, the horse is bent and flexed differently in the half pass right than he is in the left shoulder-in, but the same legs are crossing—the left legs in front of the right legs. A rider should introduce the half pass in this manner.

When a rider trains the shoulder-in and half pass, he must maintain a nice, flowing rhythm and a good amount of impulsion. The horse must always learn to go forward and sideways. Again it is very important for the

Figure 1.48

This rider had trouble executing this pirouette. The horse rocked back too far and stepped onto both hind legs thus breaking the rhythm of the canter. In this situation a horse will appear to lift his body up and down like a rocking horse due to the exaggerated elevation of the head and lowering of the croup.

Figure 1.49

An exaggerated lifting and lowering of the head, neck, and croup can also be seen here in Florencio 2. (Normally this "rocking horse" motion is only seen in horses that are performing a pirouette incorrectly). The major difference between the two horses is the speed at which they are traveling forward. The horse in fig. 1.48 cantered on the last activity with his hind legs (the horse has stopped the hind legs). Florencio 2 is cantering forward at great speed as he lengthens his stride. It will be interesting to observe Florencio 2's canter as he collects more.

Figure 1.50

Sometimes Klaus Balkenhol would instruct the riders to half halt in the shoulder-in or half pass using weight and the outside rein. The object was to shorten the horse's strides and increase the activity of the hind legs during the lateral exercise. The horses responded with a few very active, short steps and then went forward into the collected trot again. Riders had to maintain the rhythm and the line and also maintain the bend and positioning of the horse. When the riders performed this properly, the horses worked more actively as the impulsion increased. The horses also maintained a nice trot rhythm. Impulsion always came in two parts: one part work, one part relaxation.

Figure 1.51

Klaus Balkenhol, assisted by George Williams and Volker Bromman, addresses the Global Dressage Forum. Mr. Balkenhol emphasized the importance of correct and classical training for young horses. In particular he talked about not pushing young horses to produce overly sensational gaits. This form of training causes too many young horses to retire early—they can't take the mental and physical pressure.

Figure 1.52

Klaus Balkenhol demonstrates proper leading and presenting of yearlings and two-year-old horses. He stated that some handlers will artificially elevate the neck of a young horse, which causes a hollowing of the horse's back. The handlers hope to show off a reaching front leg and shoulder, but this artificial elevation blocks proper action of the hind leg. Unfortunately, horses at this age are very impressionable; they often carry these bad habits into more advanced work as they mature.

rider to keep a good rhythm; he must avoid introducing rhythm faults in the lateral work. Rhythm faults happen mostly when a rider forces a horse to move sideways. These problems are difficult to correct.

What are common mistakes in the lateral work?

Shoulder-in, haunches in, renvers, and half pass are lateral schools, or lessons according to classical dressage. Leg-yielding is only a basic teaching exercise. Often horses in the lateral schools do not carry enough weight on the hind legs. Many are not bent properly through the length of their body. Another common mistake is to see horses that are tilting or twisting at the poll; they are lacking in *durchlässigkeit*[9].

These horses will usually have problems with the contact. Through this come a lot of rhythm faults.

When do you start to train flying changes?

Flying changes are also a question of talent and ability in the horse. Riding a flying change is a question of impulsion and balance. A horse with natural gifts in these areas will learn flying changes easily. Riding a change is a matter of shifting balance from one lead to the next. A horse with a quick hind leg will find this easier than a horse with a slow hind leg. Most problems with changes occur when the hind leg is too slow, when the horse doesn't have a good inner impulsion.

A horse must learn to change while maintaining *losgelassenheit*, the supple looseness in his body. Many four-year-old horses do flying changes very well. The flying change is one of the most natural of lessons. Just watch young horses in the paddock. They jump easily from one canter to the next. Therefore, the flying change is easy to teach in a system of natural equitation.

Problems begin when riders flex or even bend too much into the new direction; the horse must learn to canter straight for the change or even flexed a little to the new outside. It is important for an experienced rider to teach a young horse flying changes or for a trained horse to teach an inexperienced rider.

In summary, train changes when the horse begins to offer them. Never train changes with violence or force. Horses offer changes after they understand collection, that is, the half halts. The horse also has to understand the leg aids. He must be familiar with the language of the rider. Then the horse is ready to learn flying changes.

How do you usually train changes? Which figures and lines do you use?

After the horse is familiar with the aids of the rider, the legs, the weight, and the hands, after the horse is familiar with lateral work; and if this horse does not show a lot of talent for changes, then I train the changes on the long side. I canter one or two meters from the rail on the inside track parallel to the long side. The horse will want to drift back to the rail. In this moment when I feel the horse trying to get back to the rail, when I feel his balance change, I ask for the flying change. Horses have an easy time changing at this moment.

I don't believe in training changes over poles on the ground. Many horses that learn by this method will change late behind. This can become a long-term problem. It is important for a horse to learn to change correctly from the start. He must learn to change with his hind and front legs at the same time.

---

[9] Literally translated, the compound noun means through-allowing-ness. In other words the horse is sufficiently *losgelassen*, or supple and loose, that he allows the aids of the rider to go through his body. The interesting distinction in both of these compound nouns is the word "allow." This implies that the horse has a choice and once more reflects the prevailing concept of a partnership between horse and rider in the German dressage language. You don't make a horse supple. If you ride well, a horse will allow a supple looseness into his way of going.

Figures 1.53–1.54

Klaus Balkenhol trains Laredo to piaffe (top) and passage (bottom). Note the quiet, relaxed contact with the horse's mouth. Mr. Balkenhol's legs hang relaxed at the horse's sides. The muscles of the horse are working but not tense. Observe the greater degree of engagement involved in the piaffe. Laredo's hind legs close under his body and he lowers his croup much more while piaffing; the distance between his hind and front feet is shorter, an indicator of the extreme engagement involved.

If I have an older horse that doesn't know changes, then I can also try collecting him on a small circle in the middle of the arena. From this collection I change rein, and as I feel the horse changing his balance into the new direction, I ask for the change. There are many variations of patterns. One must try different patterns with different horses and figure out which pattern motivates the horse the best.

When is a horse ready to learn piaffe?

When the horse offers it. Sometimes when I collect a horse and ride the half halts, the horse will offer piaffe or the passage. For example, the five-year-old that I rode today was excited last week, and he began to piaffe. I encouraged this. I rewarded him. I then walked around the arena and came back to the same spot. The horse piaffed

Figure 1.55

Klaus Balkenhol schools Pan Am Gold Medal horse Lucky Tiger in the piaffe. During the course of each session, Balkenhol sat on several of the horses. The session was quite long; each upper-level horse was out for about an hour. Each horse got several walk breaks, which were always ridden on a loose rein. If Mr. Balkenhol wanted to school a horse, he would have the student warm up the horse, then he would ride; the student would finish the session by feeling the changes in the horse after Mr. Balkenhol had ridden. "The students must learn what it feels like to ride a horse that is loose in the back with these muscles working properly."

Mr. Balkenhol uses the interaction of his weight and his legs to create the half halt, which works in rhythm with the horse. He effectively regulates how much he allows his back to follow the horse. As he sits steadier and quieter, still following but ever so slightly against the motion, the horse responds by compressing and collecting his stride. But this is subtle. Too much stiffness or bracing would force the horse's back to hollow. Too much relaxation would preclude any influence and could lead to a sloppy position and a loss of balance. In the proper amounts, the horse and rider work together in artistic efficiency. Dressage becomes a language of motion.

again. Usually I try to find a situation where the horse will piaffe, like out on the trail. When you are heading home, the horses will often get excited. Sometimes they offer the piaffe or passage. When this happens, I reward the horse, then turn him around and walk away from home. I turn him around again and come back to the same spot where the horse offered the piaffe the first time, and I encourage him to do the same. The horse will then perform this lesson again. Of course, the horse must become secure in this lesson. The horse is not allowed to be pushed or forced to learn this.

Figures 1.56–1.59

These four pictures represent a common mistake when horses learn the pirouette. The horse rocks back too far on the hind legs, behind the rider, and loses the canter rhythm. The hind legs stop.

Figures 1.60–1.63

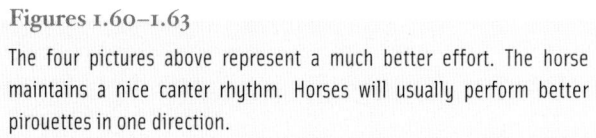

The four pictures above represent a much better effort. The horse maintains a nice canter rhythm. Horses will usually perform better pirouettes in one direction.

Do you teach piaffe or passage first?

According to classical dressage I try to train piaffe first. I half halt the horse back in a diagonal footfall into the piaffe. However, with some horses, especially ones that have not been trained to piaffe correctly, I find it better to train piaffe out of the passage. There are also other horses, usually those of a nervous type, that begin to piaffe spontaneously, even though they have no training for piaffe. Riders should reward these horses. Then they know how to piaffe. They will usually piaffe well for their whole lives. It is important for riders to realize that this is a talent that should be encouraged. The riders shouldn't turn the horse around or make him do something else which would discourage the piaffe. Most of the horses that offer a spontaneous piaffe will always piaffe correctly. They take weight onto their haunches and pick up their feet in diagonal pairs. If the rider discourages the spontaneous piaffe, then these horses begin to piaffe on the forehand.

Some horses, especially those that have learned to carry weight on the hind legs without being active, must learn piaffe from passage. The rider shortens the passage until the horse passages on the spot. At this time it is very, very important for the rider to teach the horse to be active with the hind legs, so the horse is no longer passaging on the spot, so he takes more weight onto the haunches, becomes more active and begins to piaffe. When a horse learns this engagement and activity in the piaffe, then the transitions from the passage to piaffe and from the piaffe to passage can also be ridden correctly. Problems often occur when horses piaffe too much on the forehand and don't take enough weight onto the haunches. These horses cannot execute the transitions properly. Horses that have problems in the transitions between piaffe and passage are usually not piaffing correctly.

What are some common mistakes?

The greater the amounts of collection, the finer the aids have to be. The balance becomes much finer also. When the horse is moving on the spot, the horse must be tuned into very fine aids. The leg and the hand must be used with great sensitivity, precision, and timing. This is true in all of the very collected movements, the piaffe, passage, and the pirouettes. The aids must be very, very fine. It is easy for the rider to upset the balance. The rider must not use strong aids. Too many riders force these movements. The horses are not supple and properly schooled.

Often one sees horses trip or loose the rhythm. One sees them cross the legs or balance themselves from side to side with wide hind legs. These are all problems with impulsion in the haunches; these horses are not working from back to front and thinking forward. A horse must be thinking forward in the piaffe. This doesn't mean that the horse should be strong in the hand. The horse should take a light contact with the rider's hand. If the horse has learned to collect correctly through proper half halts, he has an understanding of what will be expected of him in the piaffe. He will think forward and remain straight. His haunches will carry weight and remain active. He will remain light in the hand. The transitions will be correct. These transitions are a good indicator of the correctness in a piaffe. If the horse steps out of the piaffe with a big step, it means that the horse wasn't carrying his weight on his haunches with enough activity; he was on the forehand in piaffe. This horse loses impulsion in the transition into passage. A horse that is piaffing correctly will always think forward and keep good impulsion.

How do you train pirouettes?

First it is important to remember that with all of these lessons that require a great amount of collection, the

Figure 1.64

One can really appreciate the difficulty of a pirouette when observing the footfall in the canter with high-speed photography. These pictures were taken at 8.5 frames per second, so the steps here happen faster than the blink of an eye. Additionally, one of the most important aspects of a pirouette, a nice flowing rhythm, is impossible to see when looking at pictures. Above, Robin just finishes his stride as the left front is about to hit the ground.

Figure 1.65

As the canter stride begins again, Robin lifts his right hind leg. Notice in the pirouette canter that the right hind lifts off the ground while the remaining legs stay on the ground. This differs from a normal canter, where the new moment of suspension begins with three of the legs lifting off of the ground.

Figure 1.66

Robin lifts the diagonal pair of legs, the inside hind and the outside front. His right hind is still in the air.

Figure 1.67

The left hind and the right front are in the air, but the right hind and left front remain on the ground. At this moment the horse looks as if he is beginning to piaffe, since he appears to be working with diagonal pairs of legs.

Figure 1.68

As you can see here, the inside hind strikes before the outside front. This is normal in pirouettes; however, if the dissociation becomes too great, the horse will acquire an exaggerated rocking motion. This could lead to the horse stopping with the hind legs if the rider does not ride forward.

Figure 1.69

Robin is about to end his stride. The inside front is in the air. Remember that this canter would appear to be a normal three-beat without high-speed photography. However, observing what the horse actually has to do with his legs in a pirouette creates an appreciation for the difficulty of this movement.

horse must be strong enough and have a sufficient understanding of the aids. The horse must be strong in his muscles, tendons, and the rest of his body so he can perform these movements.

After these conditions are met, then I begin by shortening the strides on the long side by using half halts. The horse takes more weight on his haunches and learns to remain active. Later I begin to shorten on curved lines, and finally I shorten while moving the horse sideways a little.

It is important that the horse understands what is expected of him. The rider must be very clear with his aids. The horse should learn to do the pirouette without tension, without trying too hard, so that this difficult lesson becomes easy. The pirouette is the most collected movement of the canter, and it requires a great deal of strength for the horse to perform properly.

Horses must learn to perform a pirouette on the spot. They must learn to wait for the rider and not start too early. Horses must learn to jump through with the hind legs in the canter, to stay active in a three-beat canter.

What are some common mistakes?

Common mistakes include not flexing the horse enough to the inside and also horses that slip into a canter that is flat and has little expression. Of course, it is easier for horses to do a pirouette in a flat canter, and this can be used to teach a horse how to do a pirouette, but then the rider must strive to train an expressive, active canter by riding forward and sideways as the horse pirouettes.

Another common mistake is that the hind end falls out; the horse turns in its middle instead of on its haunches. Sometimes the horse falls to the inside and turns too fast. The rider can no longer control the pirouette. It is important in this case for the rider to be able to collect his horse's stride and ride forward again without losing control, so the horse never throws himself to the inside over the inside shoulder. Also horses will sometimes stop cantering with the hind legs. They must learn to keep a lively canter that does not become tense.

ERNST HOYOS

Brief Bio

Ernst Hoyos made a jump that few have managed. He came from a background of the classical riding tradition at the Spanish Riding School in Vienna, Austria. He now resides in the heart of the competitive dressage world, in Germany. The School in Vienna has been in existence for over 400 years, but few of these trainers have made their mark in the world of competitive dressage. According to Mr. Hoyos, most riders at this school are very involved in their performances and are not interested in show riding. Ernst Hoyos bucked this trend and is now recognized by many as one of the top trainers in competitive dressage.

Many of the world's best riders have sought the experienced eye and natural genius of Ernst Hoyos, including World Champion and many-time Olympic team gold medalist, Ulla Salzgeber. Additional riders who have benefited greatly from his instruction include Olympic team bronze medalist Lisa Wilcox and Martina Hannöver-Sternbeg. However, Mr. Hoyos is a private man who would rather not compile a long list of riders who have sought his expertise.

Figure 2.1

The horse stretches well over his topline, which helps his hind legs to engage and lift his shoulders. Note the relaxation and expression in the horse's trot. Extension is a test of the engagement in the collection. If the collection is ridden properly, then the extension comes easily. Engagement also gives the rider a smoother place to sit, since the horse travels lighter on his feet. This enables the rider to sit relaxed in the saddle with his legs quiet, long, and loose. Riders who grip and hold with their legs in the extension prevent the horse from engaging its hindquarters; such riders suffer a bone-jarring ride. Engage the horse's hindquarters first, and then ride the extension.

General Questions

Why do you ride?

I grew up with horses. We had a Thoroughbred breeding farm and we also bred Icelandic horses. I rode the Icelandic horses more at first. Then I began to ride three-day events with the Thoroughbreds that were too slow for the racetrack. I had these horses for the sport of eventing. As I grew older, my enthusiasm for riding grew also. Then, at the age of seventeen, I went to the Spanish Riding School.

What makes a good rider?

A good rider can feel his way into a horse very quickly. He knows what a horse needs. He must establish harmony between horse and rider. He must not wait for the horse to do this. How much or how little of an aid does a horse need? How can he teach this horse to respond to lighter aids? How can he motivate this horse? The good rider quickly gains the trust and confidence of the horse, because the horse understands his aids.

How does one learn this?

Of course with experience one learns more about feel. But a rider must be born with a basic, good understanding of the horse. Then it becomes possible to learn every day. A rider must always ask himself the question, "How do I reach the point in an easier way when the horse understands what I want?"

A rider also learns through instruction. When a rider receives good instruction from good trainers, he hears, "There, that is right, now you need to develop that feel." The rider learns through a lot of individual lessons.

What makes a great rider?

One who has a lot of feel, a lot of balance. One who can really ride a test well and has good nerves so he doesn't lose too many points in the show arena. Many good riders aren't good show riders. But the most important thing is that the rider has to understand his horse. He has to understand how much riding a horse needs. He can't ride or train the horse too hard. A rider has to be able to improve the quality of the gaits under saddle by developing the proper muscles in the horse; horses move beautifully without riders. Too much or too little work will not develop these muscles.

What makes a good trainer?

A good trainer has to have an eye, an eye that serves both the horse and the rider. He has to do this simultaneously. When I teach, I always think a little more about the well-being of the horse. I correct the rider first, and through the rider I correct the horse. That is the style of my training, how I train horses. But I always start with the rider. Through this, I make the horse better. This is my principle.

What physical and mental qualities are most important for a rider to develop in order to advance?

A rider should have a good sense of balance so he doesn't need his hands to balance; instead he must balance on his seat. A rider should be very fit. His condition should be good enough that he can always help the horse to perform better. He should be able to ride double the amount that is required. A tired rider makes a lot of mistakes. He becomes a heavy burden for the horse to carry. Mentally, he

Figure 2.2

Ernst Hoyos riding the stallion Royal Diamond on the passage volte at Gestüt Vorwerk. "I use my outside rein to guide the shoulder of the horse onto the circle. I think of my outside rein like the wall of the track. A rider should flex and loosen the horse with a soft inside rein. But when he lets go, the outside rein keeps the horse on the circle. To shorten a horse, I use my diagonal aids, my inside leg and my outside rein."

Note the loose inside rein as Ernst Hoyos gives slightly with his inside hand. The horse maintains a nice inside bend, as well as good cadence and expression in the passage. Ernst Hoyos's legs hang loosely. His spurs do not touch the horse's sides and his heels are down. "A rider who grips with the upper thigh will stop the horse. He will interfere with the energy in the horse's back. Often these riders will then use the calf to try to get a forward reaction. The rider doesn't realize that he is asking for two different things. Also, a rider must breathe from the bottom of his stomach. A rider who breathes only in the chest will be tight in the upper body. When a rider is tight in the upper body, he will be tight everywhere. He will be too tight to get a horse to go forward from a relaxed seat. He will not be able to get a response from a weight aid. A cramped, tight rider will be unable to effectively guide his horse."

2.3

2.4

2.5

2.6

Figures 2.3–2.7

Ernst Hoyos rides the trot half pass. "I begin to train the half pass on the *volte*. This teaches the horse to bend its entire body. The horse bends his body from my weight and leg position; my inside leg is forward, my outside leg is back. I gymnasticize and bend the neck with small inside half halts and then I am soft. This supples and loosens the neck. I think of freeing the inside shoulder by softening on the inside rein so the shoulder grows and stretches forward. If I am too strong with the inside rein, I block the shoulder. The outside rein guides the horse on the circle. I can let go with the inside rein, and the horse will remain on the circle. The outside rein is like the wall of the track. I ride the half pass in the same manner. I can change the amount of bend during the half pass, or I can let go with the inside rein, but the outside rein guides the outside shoulder of the horse across the line." Note that Ernst Hoyos releases the outside driving aid. His spur is passive.

has to be balanced. For example, if he gets angry too fast, then he will be unjust to the horses. One never manages to be perfectly fair, but if the rider is good natured, then he can help the horses to perform better and to learn.

How would you define a successful day in the training of a horse?

When we make a few steps forward. When we progress a few steps. I can't expect to make big leaps, only to add a little bit. When the horse is happy, and he

Figure 2.8

Gestüt Tasdorf, the training and breeding farm where Ernst Hoyos works and keeps his horses. The German breeding farms are unsurpassed in producing horses for both dressage and jumping. The science and record keeping behind this program have been emulated by many countries.

Figure 2.9

A glimpse inside the stallion barn at Gestüt Tasdorf.

learned a little bit, then that is a nice feeling, when I see a little bit of progress. There isn't always progress. Sometimes you don't move forward. Sometimes you must take a step backwards in the training. But the nicest thing in training is when you have a little success, that the horse has understood you. He has progressed and is content in his work. These are the nicest days.

You must motivate and develop a horse like you build a big mosaic. You add a little piece here and there. You build until the picture is done.

When is a horse ready to advance?

That is also a difficult situation. If you have ridden your horse up to a certain point where he is prepared to learn, you still cannot think of achieving the upcoming lesson in any complete form right away. Then the rider is ready to teach the horse to learn more.

If we want to achieve perfection immediately, we cause a lot of damage. The horse will become afraid of new lessons. This tension will make it more difficult for the horse to learn. Always proceed with little steps and don't skip over things. I'll repeat, don't skip steps. We must build very slowly; then both the horse's mind and body join in making progress. This will keep the attitude of the horse fresh.

When has a horse reached its limit?

First I'll talk about this question in relation to the daily work and then in relation to the horse's overall ability.

When I notice in the daily work that everything is getting difficult, then I must change my focus to another goal, or quit for the day. Otherwise, I will just make the horse difficult to train. He will no longer learn new things willingly. Either he doesn't understand me, or his body is not ready yet for what I am asking.

When I think about the overall ability, the horse may not be a Grand Prix horse. There are good small tour horses [Prix St. George and Intermediate I] who can learn the Grand Prix lessons, but who don't have the ability to show Grand Prix. It is better to leave these horses at the levels where they perform better, like in the small tour, rather than ask too much of their minds or bodies by doing Grand Prix. The rider should never expect more quality out of the horse than is there, which is often a question of misplaced ambition from the trainer or the rider that takes the horse to this point.

Then such a horse gets pushed and can no longer perform even in the small tour?

Right. They have lost a quality in their gaits because they no longer want to present themselves. They have lost their shine; have been trained too much and endlessly drilled. Pressured like a dog. This is not the goal and meaning in the education of a horse. It is always good when I can train a horse to do everything, but many times it is not important to show all of these movements at a competition.

Do you think that horses learn something good from performing these lessons even if they will never learn them very well? For example, in the piaffe, does a horse get something out of piaffing even if he will never get a high score at the piaffe?

Nearly all horses can learn every lesson in a Grand Prix, as long as they don't have problems in their education. They can learn to understand these lessons, but if they ever reach the quality to show Grand Prix, that is another question. But almost every horse can learn every lesson. Sometimes a trainer has to search for a different way, but with patience, both horse and rider can learn a lot.

Figure 2.10

Long-time student and Olympic bronze medalist, Lisa Wilcox is shown on her way to winning the Prix St. Georges on Jazz Time 2 with a 72 percent. Note the steady contact with the snaffle rein and the well-developed and working topline muscles. Lisa sits relaxed and upright in the saddle as the horse steps forward in a ground-covering stride. "Riders who are tight in the upper body cannot guide their horse with their seat," says Ernst Hoyos. The hind legs are engaged and carrying. Lisa's legs seems to hover over the horse's side. Of course, she is indeed touching the horse, but she is never in the way of the performance. "A rider must always do everything possible not to interfere with the motion of the horse," explains Ernst Hoyos. "She must enhance the gaits and bring the quality to the surface, but not get in the way."

"A rider who squeezes with the leg constantly will cause the horse to tighten, to not want to move. This can become a problem. This rider must use less leg, and the horse will want to move more forward. For horses that have developed this stiffness to a great degree, it may require the rider to take his legs completely off of the horse for a few strides and then slap the horse with the inside of his boots. But this must be done with the flat or inside part of the leg." In other words, the toes must be pointed forward. "The rider should not kick the horse with the spur. Soon when the rider lifts his legs away from the horse he will get a forward reaction. This starts to train the horse to listen to the lightest of aids."

This is very ironic. A rider who uses too much leg will feel that he needs more leg to get the horse to go forward. The only way to break this vicious cycle would be to do the exact opposite of what he thinks is right—to use less leg. This situation applies to other dressage lessons as well. It stresses the importance that every rider needs an outside eye, somebody with experience on the ground. The top riders seek the experienced eyes of the great dressage masters.

Figures 2.11–2.14
Every rider should strive for this level of excellence even when executing simple lessons. Try making your aids invisible when riding walk-trot-walk transitions.

When does a rider need a new horse?

He needs a new horse, if he notices that he needs more quality in the gaits, or if his horse is too old. But to be successful in this sport, a rider must have two to four horses. Every two years, he must buy a new young horse. Otherwise the chance that bad luck will strike is too great, and a lame horse will take a rider out of the sport. If he has a new horse coming along, he will not have such of a hard fall.

2.15

2.16

2.17

2.18

Figures 2.11–2.19

Ernst Hoyos schooling the piaffe on Royal Diamond.

"In the piaffe, I wish that I would see more *losgelassenheit*. Of course, this can only happen if the riders learn not to use so much spur and learn to sit quietly. Most riders are more active than their horses. The test of a well-educated horse is to piaffe from invisible aids. Riders must learn that the more that they get tight and push, the harder it is for the horse to perform. They must train self-carriage in the piaffe."

Figure 2.20

Ernst Hoyos coaches a student at the Bremen Grand Prix.

How would you define a great horse?

A great horse has to have three super, basic gaits and a beautiful exterior. If this horse is good in his head, then this horse is great, he is perfect.[10]

Did you have a favorite horse?

A favorite horse is the one who understands me the best, as a person, during the training process. One tends to like this horse more. But one is not allowed to search for a favorite. A professional has too many horses. None should be treated with less kindness than the others. This could be very unfair. While keeping this in mind, the horse that one has had the most success with often becomes a horse that one feels very close to. This is automatic. This happens more with women than with men; at least we don't

---

[10] There is a story of a magical horse Satori. In a state of deep and enlightened meditation, the lucky one achieves an illuminated ride through the universe on the back of this all powerful beast. But what if this Satori really appeared? Would we only succeed in dragging him down to our level? Maybe he is already here.

show it the same way that women do. We may feel the same way about a horse, but we don't demonstrate our feelings. This is a difference between men and women. They kiss, pet, and hug their horses more than men. This is a comparison.

What is excellence?

Excellence is when a horse learns every lesson like a champion. Of course, this never happens. Every horse has strong and weak points. But if a horse's weak points can be improved through training so they reach a very high quality of work, then this horse achieves excellence. If during the daily work, a horse achieves a "9" in many of his lessons, that is excellence. I'm not speaking in terms of a "10" because the judges only reward certain riders with a "10." Also, there are some horses that work and achieve more than one would expect from looking at their conformation. They try hard and overcome many weaknesses. This is also a form of excellence: A horse that always tries hard.

If you could change one thing about the world of competitive dressage, what would it be? What is the biggest disadvantage of competitive dressage?

The hardest thing with competing in dressage is that we are dependent upon the objectivity of the judges. Maybe we need another system of judging; one that would judge more horses correctly and one that would judge more riders correctly. I would like to change something in this area.

Would you do this by training judges better?

Train judges better, yes. However, I would also like to diminish the huge responsibility of the individual judges. I would like to make their scores count less by having more judges at the arena. Then we could scratch the highest and lowest marks. With only five judges determining the score, each score has a big impact on the results. One judge's bad marks can hurt. It doesn't mean that these marks are given deliberately. Even judges can have bad days. But these bad days, in and of themselves, can ruin a lot of good training and diminish the perceived quality in a horse. There is a mistake in this system. That is the problem.

Does this also relate indirectly to a theme that we discussed earlier, the problem of judges wanting to see ever more sensational horses?

That's right. Many horses that are ridden in this manner [getting pushed too hard] are judged very high even though they haven't earned it. There are usually problems with regularity and rhythm with these horses that are so stressed, but many judges seem to ignore this. Other horses that are ridden well end up in the middle but should be placed higher. This takes the motivation away from many riders, so they don't continue to work. Another consequence is that many horses break down at an early age. But this is a very difficult theme in our sport that is not easy to solve. There are no easy answers.

What do you think about the young horse classes? For example, the World Championships for five- and six-year-olds; do you think that these horses get worked too hard?

I believe that most of them are pushed too much. These horses in this young age end up being too powerful. Their quality is peaked at too young of an

Figure 2.21
Midway through the warm-up at the Bremen Grand Prix.

age. Much of the riding is artificial, a type of tension-riding to get the big gaits. When the tension-riding is done well, then you don't notice the tension so much, but you see the extreme movement in the trot and canter. This type of riding isn't healthy for the horse. Most of these horses have worked so hard that they have a tough time later if they make it to Grand Prix. Many of these horses get so sour that they never perform with this intensity again. Their minds can't take it.

So, even if the body stays sound, there is a good chance that the mind won't?

Yes. The danger for the young horses **at most** championships is that the judging rewards **the most** spectacular movement. These horses get **placed first**. The foundation of good quality in a horse's **gaits** and training is ignored. As I said before, many **of these** spectacular horses show irregularities **and rhythm** faults. The canter begins to look like a **four-beat**. There are irregularities in the trot, and **the walk** becomes lateral. This is not a good foundation for later work. The classical school of riding is founded upon rhythm.

These faults should be penalized much more in these classes. Then much of this type of riding would diminish. Much of the riding in these classes is a form of business-riding, where horses are just tools or things that are used to make money. These horses are marketed for high prices. I have nothing against people earning or spending money, quite the opposite. If these horses go on and do well, then everything is fine. But it is very probable that they will not trot so well or perform in such a spectacular manner as eight- or nine-year-olds. Then there are many disappointments. Some investors are convinced that if they buy a champion six-year-old, that this horse will be a champion nine-year-old. Usually this is not the case. In this type of competition, no horse is a champion of every level. This type of business-riding causes a lot of damage. That is an obvious fact.

What is the best thing about competitive dressage? Are there good influences from competition?

Yes, but I would like to see more changes. If judges watched in the warm-up arena, then they could see which work is genuine and which work shouldn't be a part of our beautiful sport. Judges could penalize or eliminate riders who are too rough on their horses. A few riders are overly harsh on their horses in the warm-up. Then they go into the show arena and ride like angels. If there were warm-up judges, the scores could reflect not only the five minutes in the dressage arena, but they would also show how these five minutes are prepared. Then we would be much fairer and just to the living being that is the horse.

So you believe that a judge should stand at the warm-up and observe?

Yes, but more than one. First, it must be decided what is allowed to happen in the warm-up. Then the judges could reprimand or even disqualify riders who violate the rules. Riders could no longer prepare a horse with very severe aids and then ride soft and sweet in front of the judges.

These measures would be correct for our time. Many won't want to hear what I have to say, but I'm not trying to make any more friends; I haven't ever tried to do this. I just say it like it is.

What is the best thing that comes from showing?

The possibility that a great partnership will develop. A rider and his horse can climb to the top of the Grand Prix, or no matter the level that they achieve; they can be partners through each step of progress. In this process the understanding between the horse and rider team becomes increasingly better. That is a big advantage of this sport.

Perhaps the "warm-up" judges should try to see if a partnership exists between the horse and rider, or see if the horse is punished and forced into subservience?

Yes. They shouldn't just see if they have the "happy horse" in the competition arena, and then behind the doors, something else entirely different is going on.[11]

---

[11] Ernst Hoyos referred to a suggestion that the FEI judges not only score the test, but they watch the horse's reactions and try to determine if the horse appears to be happy, hence we would have a "Happy Horse" collective mark at the bottom of the test. According to several trainers with whom I have spoken, many judges would be shocked by the preliminary scores that they gave for happy horses, if they saw how these horses were prepared. Judges have so much to observe and quantify, I don't believe that adding a happy horse score will be effective in curbing warm-up abuse.

Figure 2.22
Ernst Hoyos riding the passage on Royal Diamond at Gestüt Vorwerk. Note Ernst Hoyos's quiet position, with his heels down. He *allows* the horse to develop self-carriage by using aids only when necessary to make a change. Each aid must have a goal of making a change. Each aid must have a moment when it begins and a moment when it ends. If a horse doesn't respond in a way that the rider anticipated, then the rider must rethink how he applies his aids and why he is not communicating effectively with his horse. The horse should never be blamed for not understanding what the rider wants.

What was your greatest setback?

Well, that is a question that I find hard to answer . . .

I guess if I look back about fifteen years and look at the horses that I was schooling then . . . If I could only have known then what I know now. If only I had the same abilities and knowledge back then that I have now, I could have ridden these horses much better. If I look at a specific problem that I was having with a horse, I know now that I could solve that problem and do much better by the horse. Only back then, I wasn't advanced enough.

That was probably because . . . you see these things first when it is too late.

When I look ahead with this knowledge, it helps me to have patience. I work on improving my riding to improve my horses.

What was your greatest victory?

One of the most beautiful things is when you train a young horse and bring him up to Grand Prix. I have done this many times. That is really something beautiful. It is really a victory. It is more than a competition victory. It is an inner contentment that I get when I know that I have accomplished my work.

What was your most memorable ride?

Sometimes you have a ride where everything goes right, when you are ahead of the horse with the correct aids, when you feel that you can give the correct aids in your sleep, when there is a perfect harmony between horse and rider. I'm not speaking about competition rides. There were days like this even at the Spanish Riding School, and on normal training days when everything was easy, and yet the quality of everything was very high. These days are highlights for every rider. That's how it is. But one doesn't have a day like this every day, yes. But one should work toward having more of these days. That's the hard part.

What was your worst ride?

When I fail to meet any of the points that I just described. But when you have one of these days, you shouldn't beat yourself up. And you certainly shouldn't beat your horse.

Can you share a humorous experience with us?

Once when I rode at the Austrian Championships, I had a big horse. He was a very nervous type. There were five judges. When the results were posted, I was in front by a wide margin with four judges. I was in last place, also by a wide margin, with the remaining judge. Later, I asked this judge, "Why was I so far behind?" He answered, "I didn't see you give any aids. I didn't see that you were riding." At the time, I found this very funny. I guess if I would have given bigger aids and worked a little harder, I would have been placed a lot higher by this judge. We had a lot of fun with this statement.

Isn't that a strange answer?

Yes, that's true. This was a Grand Prix judge.

Do you have advice for a striving rider?

First, he has to be ambitious. Mentally, he has to be well balanced and consistent. He has to be tougher on himself than on the horse. If he gets after the horse too much, he will not get far. One must really be able to push oneself harder than one ever pushes a horse. Then, success will follow. One has to consistently follow this principle, and follow it, and follow it.

What do American dressage riders need to work on the most? What is missing in American dressage?

The Americans have too few good trainers. For many the basics are too weak. They have very good horses. They have a few good riders, but too few good trainers. They also have too few good shows, at least the type of shows that we have in Europe. That's why the Americans must always go to Europe to show and measure their skills in this type of competition. They have to learn to appreciate and celebrate this kind of show. The Americans ride tests, but that is not enough. There is a big difference between the tests that I am describing and what most Americans do. I'm speaking of the millimeter work, the exactness.

Figure 2.23

Ernst Hoyos trains the seven-year-old stallion King Arthur TSF in the piaffe. Note that Hoyos activates the horse and then sits quietly so he allows self-carriage. Riders who constantly use the spurs cause the horse to cramp and resist the harsh aids. Ironically, the bombarded horse slows his footfall, so the overly active rider feels like he needs more driving aids—less is more.

The horse will only remain active and in self-carriage when a high degree of *losgelassenheit* (loose-allowing-ness) is present.

Figure 2.24

Ernst Hoyos riding the piaffe on Royal Diamond. Is it really possible to sit that quietly on a horse? No matter what the horse did, Ernst Hoyos's feet never seemed to move. He is catlike in his balance. This was truly an example of athletic and yet quiet riding. Mr. Hoyos, like other dressage masters, has a deep respect for the horse and its motion. He is careful to not interfere as he enhances and brings the horse's natural gaits to the surface.

What do the European dressage riders need to work on the most? What is missing in European dressage?

In Europe, dressage riders need to lose the doggedness in the sport. Most here think too much about dressage as a business. Through this, we get the doggedness. This is primarily the pressure in Germany. Many find it hard to make a living. They don't develop their skills and their art like they should. They become sales riders, business riders.

We spoke about this theme earlier in regards to the young horse classes, that many of these horses get pushed too hard, that many riders extract more brilliance from a horse than the horse can give.

And many of these riders that ride in the young horse classes are not able to ride at the upper levels. They are no longer capable of acquiring the feel. There is a difference in riding.

Does something good come from these young horse classes? Or are we cutting the careers of champions short by expecting too much too soon? Are we losing potential Grand Prix champions?

If one of these horses gets put into very good hands, where not only the body can be repaired, but also the horse's mind, then there is a chance. But most trainers make the same mistake. When a horse wins the World Championships as a six-year-old, it develops too much pressure for any trainer. The horse must continually get better. This is where things get difficult. Many of these horses don't make it in the long run.

I guess the problem is that they have to win next week also, otherwise they are the defeated World Champion.

This pressure gets added to the training. I think it is better if somebody buys the fourth- or fifth-placed horse that hasn't been and will not be subjected to the same kinds of pressures. After two years, this horse will be better than the former champion.

Figure 2.25

USA Olympic bronze medalist Lisa Wilcox passaging on Royal Diamond in the Verden Grand Prix. While schooling Lisa Wilcox in the warm-up, Ernst Hoyos would sometimes say, "Left eye. When I tell her left eye, I'm referring to the flexion at the poll. I want her to flex the horse more so she can see his left eye." Lisa would slowly change the flexion slightly to the left after this comment. She used a soft series of squeezes with her left hand, and she immediately released after each squeeze.

This may sound like a relatively easy task. However, Mr. Hoyos would sometimes give this instruction when Lisa Wilcox was in the middle of a beautifully balanced piaffe. As the amount of collection increases so must the lightness of the aids. It takes a rider with a lot of feel and balance to get a horse to piaffe with a high degree of energy and engagement. Then, to make a subtle change of the flexion while maintaining all of the other good qualities is no easy task. It may be easy for a person to reach up and scratch his left ear, but try having him do that while juggling a bowling ball, an egg, and a chain saw. In Grand Prix dressage, you need to harness a horse's explosive energy, balance his body to yours by engaging the hindquarters, make sure that his back is swinging and working in a rhythmic manner, monitor that his feet are always exactly where you intend them to be, and smile—the judges are watching. You have to be able to use a firm aid when the horse wants to be a bowling ball and then in the very next instant not crush the delicate balance of the egg. Oh, and don't forget to rev the motor of the chain saw for a little excitement. Add to this the fact that the horse can switch back and forth from a bowling ball to an egg at any whim or disturbance, and you have a sport that could be called challenging—so challenging and difficult that no one ever receives a 100 percent. Usually a score between 75 percent and 80 percent will win the class. And every dressage rider has ended up with egg on his face at least once.

Figure 2.26

This young horse was startled by the noise from my motor drive. He spooked and bolted forward. Notice how Ernst Hoyos keeps his upper body in a slightly forward position. He doesn't fall backwards against the horse's back or mouth and pull. Mr. Hoyos reacts forward together with the horse while keeping his balance. He never rides what happened two seconds ago; he adjusts instantly. He maintains his independent position and keeps moving with the horse. He will calmly bring the horse back onto the aids. He builds confidence in the horse by not interfering and bracing against the horse's motion even as the horse is startled. Inexperienced riders can easily frighten a young horse by clamping and holding too much. In these situations, the horse spooks not only at the outside stimulus, he spooks at his rider. This can develop long-term problems.

It will be very interesting to watch the trends of these horses that win at the FEI classes at young ages. How do you think they will perform?

You can already see the results. There are very few horses that are champions of every level. Most young champions fall to the side at later dates. They don't hold up. They are used up. These horses should be peaked in their performance at age ten. They shouldn't even be peaked at nine, but at ten.

You mean that they should begin to show Grand Prix at age nine, but their first year should be a little easier?

Yes. Then as ten-year-olds, they should be champions. That is the goal that one normally would set according to classical dressage education.

Training Questions

YOUNG HORSE

At what age should a horse be backed?

Horses can be backed at age three, but it is important to remember that they are very immature at this age. The rider should be reasonable in the amount of work he expects from the horse. It is easy to do too much. These young horses don't need to be ridden every day. The rider can alternate days between longeing and riding.

What is the most important thing when schooling a very young horse?

The horse must find his rhythm. The most important thing is rhythm and that the horse learns to carry himself using his entire topline. Through this the horse gets more balanced, the hind legs step under more; the hind end engages without pressure from the rider. The center of gravity for horse and rider shifts toward the hind legs.

Through this work, the horse starts to develop back muscles. The neck also becomes strong in a beautiful way, but only if the horse is not forced together with strong aids from the rider.

Of course, there are many more points, but these are some of the important points when schooling a horse in the first year under saddle.

What mistakes do you often observe?

Most horses are held too much by the rider's hand. This blocks the horse's forehand so the horse can no longer sustain any impulsion. The horse is crammed together. This is more or less a violent method of riding because the horse is forced together. The horse loses the desire to present himself. He loses impulsion. Some of these horses begin to do *schwebe trab*.[12] The horse uses his legs but not his back. The legs are not lifted up and forward because the back doesn't swing. As a consequence, the horse also loses his balance.

As the horse gets older, around five years old, the rider has to be able to regulate the energy in a horse's back. For example, in the lengthenings, the horse must carry more energy in its back and will consequently have more contact in the rider's hand. But this should only be done for short periods of time. If the rider tries to hold this energy too long, then the horse will start to run forward and get rhythm faults. The goal when riding this energy into the horse's back is to not shorten the horse's neck. This happens too

Figure 2.27

Mareike Peckholz schools four-year-old Imperial. All horses start and end their work sessions with a period of walk on a long rein. "At this age the horse should accept contact and travel in a free, forward, and even rhythm. Irregularities often result from riders pressuring young horses too much. This damages the body, but it also leads to a lack of desire to perform at later ages. Horses that work too hard as youngsters lose the desire to present themselves."

---

[12] This is a trot where the horse is very tense in the back from being driven forward against the hand. The horse acquires a false cadence that approaches passage but is distinctly different because of the heightened tension in the horses's back. Sometimes this is called passage-trot in English.

Figure 2.28

The young horses are ridden forward in a nice rhythm. The horses canter straight in a slight shoulder-fore, as can be seen here with the four-year-old Imperial (who is very interested in the camera). Trot-canter transitions help to relax the horse's back, as well as many transitions within the canter.

often. When the topline doesn't stay long, then the hind end is gone.

Many times it is possible for a clever rider to shorten a horse's neck and frame and perform well in young horse classes, for example the FEI Five & Six Year Tests. But when this horse has to advance to the next level of collection, the horse has problems. We should not expect a five-year-old to trot like a seven-year-old, but it seems many judges like horses that deceive the eyes and violate the rules in a spectacular manner. Often judges ignore rhythm faults. Young horses that are presented well in this short, tense frame often win as youngsters, but they lose the desire and ability to perform at higher levels. They don't hold up in their minds or their bodies.

Also, some horses are more advanced at three or four years old than others. Every rider should know if their horse is advanced or not. Often riders make the mistake of pushing the advanced horse too much; they force more out of the horse. The rider's ambition takes over.

This is human nature. It is a byproduct of competitive riding. Nobody wants to finish last. If the judges want to reward spectacular young horses which have significant training problems, then many riders will try to force their horses to look like the ones which won.

A trainer should be able to talk to his clients and say, "Wait. Don't push your horse too hard now. Let him develop two more years, and then you will be farther along than the others." This situation is best. But many people don't have patience. They want success now.

The goal of dressage training used to be to bring a horse along as far as he could go. Times have changed.

What should the horse know at the end of the first year of training?

The horse at this age should have a basic understanding of simple aids. He should react to the leg and the hand and be able to do transitions between the walk and trot and the trot and canter. The horse should understand and be able to maintain a steady, chewing contact with the rider's hand. A horse at this age should be ridden forward in a quiet rhythm so he begins to straighten his body and step under with the hind legs, but the rider must be careful not to ask for too much engagement.

When do you begin lateral work?

I begin to train lateral work only after a horse can do a correct *volte*.[13] This is an exam for the horse that tests his ability to balance his body with his hind legs. Any rhythm faults that occur on the *volte* mean that the horse is not yet ready for lateral work. He is not capable of bending his entire body and maintaining engagement. After the horse can do a correct *volte*, he can start learning shoulder-fore. After he has developed some strength in the hindquarters, he can begin to learn haunches-in.

I noticed that the second level tests in Germany have no lateral work, but they have eight-meter circles. In the USA we are required to show shoulder-in and haunches-in.

Second level is much too early to show lateral work. Five-year-old horses are not developed enough in the haunches. They will only learn to move sideways to evade the engagement.

Do you use leg-yielding and, if so, where (in the arena)?

As a very basic exercise to teach a young horse to move off of the leg, I will use a limited amount of leg-yielding. I am against too much leg-yielding because it puts horses on the forehand. Because of this, most people make the mistake of shortening a horse's neck too much when they ride this exercise. The horse gets heavy and pulls, so the rider pulls back. The theory behind dressage is to get horses more on the haunches.

Leg-yielding is not a developing exercise. It can be used for a few steps to make a horse more responsive to the leg. In limited amounts, you can train a correct response in the horse's mind, but in the long run you must train the horse's mind to develop and use the correct muscles. You accomplish this by riding lessons like the shoulder-in, where horses must learn to think about engaging their haunches. In other words, a small amount of leg-yielding is fine, but if you use too much, it quickly becomes counterproductive.

If I use a few steps of leg-yielding, I avoid doing it along the wall with the horse's nose facing the wall. This

---

[13] The term *volte* in German means "small circle." The size of this *volte* depends on a horse's level of traning.

pushes the horse's hind legs out instead of under the horse's center of gravity. Sometimes I will leg-yield a few steps on a twenty-meter circle, but I think about getting the horse into small amount of a renvers position.

At what age do you begin to show horses?

I like to get horses out as four-year-olds. I'm not a big fan of material classes, but they serve as good learning experiences for the horse. They can also be good classes to demonstrate a horse's abilities in order to sell the horse. Some professionals must show three-year-olds in order to make a living, which is fine, but horses in training with me do not show at this young age. The temptation when showing a horse is to work the horse too hard in order to win. This can damage the horse physically and mentally.

COLLECTION

How do you begin your training sessions?

I begin work with a long session of walking on a loose rein. This is sometimes ridden by a working student. The horse must become loose and relaxed before he starts his work.

I ride many lessons in the rising trot as I begin to collect the horses. I ride shoulder-in, half pass, lengthenings, and even passage—all in the rising trot. This is for the horses back. Riders can cause a lot of damage if they tighten and brace against the horse's back. I like all of my horses to be able to do all of the trot work, except piaffe of course, in the rising trot.

Are you saying a rider should never brace against the motion of the horse?

Maybe for a half a step here and there, but not too often. Working against the horse's mouth by pulling or sitting and pushing has nothing to do with correct riding. I say this often. Of course, a rider has to be firm with the aids for short periods of time, but the whole riding system cannot be built upon a foundation of strong aids, this pushing and pulling type of riding. This causes too many horses to be retired early.

It is important for riders to ride many transitions. Not only transitions between the gaits, but also transitions within the gaits. A rider must play with the transitions and go actively forward and come back so he avoids a monotonous gait, or horses will lose the desire to go forward. Riders must always maintain the correct relationship between the leg and the hand. This is a continuing process. Most riders have their horse too strong at the poll and not reacting enough from the leg. Riders who hold too much will take away their horse's energy.

Riders must also take into consideration the temperament of the horse. Lazy or nonenergetic horses need to be worked more. They have to always do a little more than you think is enough, so they get energetic. Nervous and naturally fit horses need to work a little less, otherwise they get too fit. This can easily turn into the problem of always riding more and more. Soon these horses are working five minutes longer every day. Nervous horses should only work more right before a show so they are a little calmer. Many riders just work horses according to what the horse wants to offer. These horses end up being smarter than the riders. This happens too often. When working with horses, one has to often do the opposite of what one first thinks may be correct. Much of riding is counterintuitive.

When I ride, I use the diagonal aids to close the horse's hind legs. When I have the horse flexed to the left, I use my right rein and left leg to shorten a horse's stride and close the hind legs [bring the hind legs farther under the horse's body]. When I use my outside rein, I must come immediately with my inside leg so the horse

Figure 2.29

Ernst Hoyos demonstrates a technique to help riders learn how to place and keep their weight on the inside seat bone during the half pass: Look to the inside and down.

remains active and straight. Many riders make the mistake of half halting too much with the inside rein. This blocks the inside shoulder. It interferes with the shoulder freedom in the horses. Riders also steer too much with the inside rein. They turn by pulling on this rein.

Some riders also make the mistake of wagging a horse's head from side to side—like the tail of a dog. This is not the proper technique to flex a horse.

But all of this is not so easy. It is much easier to say than to do.

Figure 2.30

Ernst Hoyos rides Rinaldini in the half pass. The engagement and the carrying power in the hindquarters help the horse to reach forward and sideways in the lateral work. "I do not begin to teach lateral work until the horse is balanced on the *volte*. The horse must first develop sufficient engagement and carrying power on a small circle before he can move sideways. This is usually at the 'M' [third] level." The horse's back is round and up, which frees the shoulders.

Mr. Hoyos rides many lessons in the rising trot during a long warm-up phase, including shoulder-in, half pass, and even passage. "I believe that one must always be careful with a horse's back. It is also a good test to see if the horse is on the aids."

Can you describe an ideal half halt?

An ideal half halt is one that is invisible. The horse responds to invisible aids.

Do you use one form of lateral work more often than the others?

I believe the most important lateral exercise is shoulder-in. I use it in not just the trot, but also in the walk and the canter. The shoulder-in helps the horse to understand the outside rein contact and half halt. The horse develops a nice connection with the outside rein. The shoulder-in also helps to straighten the horse. It is a good lesson for both young and old horses.

Shoulder-in can be ridden on both straight and curved lines. It is a good exercise to ensure that horses never lose their balance by falling through the inside shoulder. Half pass is more attractive, but shoulder-in is one of the most important exercises.

Figure 2.31

A student of Hoyos, Frau Petra Wilm, rides her mare Attention 28 in the Bremen Grand Prix. Note the engagement of the hind leg and the power that originates from the horse's topline. The rider sits with long legs down and follows beautifully in this very big extension. Her heels are down as the horse propels himself forward in a ground-covering stride.

Which combinations of lateral work do you prefer?

One of my favorite exercises is to ride a shoulder-in, then a few steps of half pass, then again a shoulder-in. If I continue this pattern, it resembles a staircase. This exercise gymnasticizes the horse, and it is a good test to see if the horse is on the aids.

What are common mistakes in the lateral work?

Mostly I see that the inner shoulder of the horse is blocked by the rider. This happens when the rider uses too much inside rein, but also from using too much inside leg. This greatly limits the inside freedom of the shoulder. Too much of either or both of these aids causes the horse to cramp his muscles on the inside of his body. This cramped horse is unable to stretch forward with his inside front leg.

When is a horse ready to collect?

It is important never to try to teach a horse its first lessons in collection in the walk. The quality of the walk usually suffers. I believe it is easiest to teach collection in the canter. The cantering horse understands best how to take more weight on the hind legs; both hind legs are swinging forward together. This is also the easiest gait for the rider to see if the horse is carrying himself. A well-balanced and engaged canter is a pleasure to ride. The trot is more difficult, both for the horse and the rider. Because of the mechanics of the gait, the horse has a more difficult time understanding how to transfer his and the rider's weight onto the haunches. I teach collection first in the canter, then the trot, and last in the walk.

When do you start to train flying changes?

This depends upon the plans for showing the horse. If the horse is going to compete at "L" level [second level] as a five-year-old, then I avoid teaching flying changes. The horse will anticipate the flying change whenever he counter canters; the scores in the counter canter will suffer.

I usually teach my own horses the flying change first and then the counter canter. I find the flying changes easier to teach before the counter canter becomes too established, before the horse thinks that flying changes are wrong. This method should only be used by advanced riders; otherwise the quality of the counter canter will suffer.

How do you usually train changes? Which figures and lines do you use?

I usually avoid riding too much counter canter before I teach changes. I would rather teach changes before I teach counter canter. Of course, this is impossible for horses that show through the levels. They must show a lot of counter canter at "L," or second, level.

I usually start changes on a short diagonal [for example F-E]. I ride several transitions between the canter and the walk. I canter the left lead, then walk. Next I canter right, then walk. I ride several simple changes while monitoring that the horse reacts well off of the leg. The horse must respond forward easily. Then I ask for the change. This is brain work for the horse. This gets him thinking about the next lead.

For horses that have problems I use serpentines with simple changes, so they get the idea of moving from one balance to the next. We can avoid many problems when we think ahead and do exercises that teach the horse what we want. We never avoid all of the problems, but many.

When is a horse ready to learn piaffe?

I usually start to train piaffe when the horse is six. At this age the horse understands balancing on his haunches, correct lateral work, and flying changes. The horse travels in collected gaits with good self-carriage. I train piaffe in hand first. When the horse is seven, I start to train piaffe with a rider.

How do you begin to train this exercise?

I teach piaffe in hand first. The weight of the rider on the horse's back causes too much interference; horses get a little cramped or hold themselves stiff. I

Figure 2.32

Notice that Ernst Hoyos remains consistently light and relaxed in the saddle in all of the piaffe pictures. Like the jockey, the dressage rider must strive to allow the horse's natural gaits to shine with no hindrance or constraint—but in a very different position. A heavy, braced rider will smother any spark of brilliance from his equine partner. In ancient times (before modern physics) people thought a rider who sat well on a horse weighed less than a clumsy rider, even if the good rider weighed more while dismounted. The horse's light and easy carriage under the educated and soft rider produced this logical conclusion.

want a horse to remain *losgelassen*[14] when he learns to piaffe. I want to see that his tail is relaxed. Too often horses hold their tails stiff. This is a sign that the horse's back is tense.

---

[14] This has to be developed. It cannot be forced. Part of *losgelassenheit* is relaxation that resembles tranquility.

When is a horse ready to passage?

Most horses learn to passage much easier than they learn to piaffe. But if I teach passage first, then the horse has a much more difficult time learning piaffe. Often horses are too tense in the passage. If a rider pulls and pushes at the same time with strong aids, many horses will drop their backs and

Figure 2.33
The moment before a transition from the passage to piaffe on Royal Diamond.

do a *fake* passage. The steps come more from tension than from relaxation. The horse hollows and becomes strong in the rider's hands. Horses ridden in this manner experience significant difficulties in the piaffe.

After a horse is confirmed in the piaffe, I start to train passage. This is the classical approach to train these lessons.

What are some common mistakes?

A very common mistake is to see that the rider is more active than the horse. These riders inevitably use too much spur. A rider can briefly use the spur to activate the horse, but the rider cannot poke a horse into piaffe. The longer the spur stays in the horse, the slower the horse moves his legs. If somebody stuck a finger in a person's side with significant pressure, wiggled it

Figures 2.34–2.37

Ernst Hoyos uses his aids to activate the horse, and then he sits quietly and follows the motion. The horse learns to piaffe by himself, under the rider. Only in this way can the horse maintain sufficient *losgelassenheit* to keep the activity in his hind legs. Many riders confuse a lack of *losgelassenheit* with laziness. However, an overuse of driving aids by the rider will make both of these problems worse.

around, and kept it there for many moments, the person would tighten and cramp his body; he would be in pain. He would lose all relaxation and suppleness. His feet would move slower and the rhythm would be lost. The same thing happens with a horse.

This mistake is much too common. Riders guilty of this do not do their horses justice.

What do you wish that you would see more often?

I wish that I would see more *losgelassenheit*. Of course, this can only happen if the riders learn not to use so much spur and learn to sit quietly. Most riders are more active than their horses. The test of a well-educated horse is to piaffe from invisible aids. Riders must learn that the more that they get tight and push, the harder it is for the horse to perform. They must train self-carriage in the piaffe.

I have never met a rider with so much feel and timing that he could use his spurs every step, exactly in time to the horse's rhythm. I can't do it. Some people must think that they have this ability, even though they obviously do not; I see this mistake too often. These riders need to understand the theory of self-carriage better. They need to learn to allow their horses to piaffe with no help from the rider.

How do you train pirouettes?

One method I like to use is to start with a walk pirouette. When the horse is in the walk pirouette, I ask for the canter, and I continue the pirouette. The horse does a piece of the pirouette in the walk and a piece in the canter. This helps the horse to understand what is expected of him.

What are some common mistakes?

One of the most common mistakes is that the rider only thinks about moving the hind end of the horse around. This makes the job of the horse very difficult. A rider should think about having the horse in a good frame and then turning the head, the shoulders, the middle of the horse, and lastly the haunches. Riders who push the haunches around too much make the horse's job much more difficult.

Pirouettes are not so difficult for horses, but riders make them difficult. Many riders fail to realize that the horse has four legs and the rider two. This may seem obvious, but the concept is difficult to grasp in very collected movements. Riders think about turning on their own feet, so they address the hind end of the horse and forget about the front end.

DR. UWE SCHULTEN-BAUMER

Brief Bio

Perhaps one of the most successful trainers in the history of modern dressage, Dr. Schulten-Baumer is not one to rest on his laurels. Nearing the age of eighty, he and his stepdaughter Ellen have five top Grand Prix horses in their barn. Dr. Schulten-Baumer purchased four of these horses at auctions as three-year-olds; the other is a horse that they acquired as a rehabilitation project. Additionally, many youngsters are showing promise as they move up the levels. On her top Grand Prix horse, Ellen recently won a coveted place on the German Team at Aachen, where she helped to win the team silver medal.

Dr. Schulten-Baumer's first major success as a trainer came when his son, Dr. Schulten-Baumer Jr., won the individual silver medal and a team gold in the 1978 World Championships; he was one point shy of the individual gold. He went on to win the individual silver medal and a team gold at the 1980 Alternate Olympics. Next, Dr. Schulten-Baumer's training helped Nicole Uphoff to win her two Olympic individual gold medals and two team gold medals. Another of his long-time students, Isabell Werth, was the Olympic individual silver medalist in the 1992 Barcelona Games (behind Nicole who won the gold), and the Olympic individual and team gold medalist in the 1996 Olympics (she has three Olympic equestrian gold medals, right behind Nicole's four). Additionally Isabell and Nicole were both European and World Champions. Dr. Schulten-Baumer's students have won more Olympic gold medals than most countries have won in their entire equestrian Olympic history.

A modest man, Dr. Schulten-Baumer refrains from giving generalized advice to the public or expressing strong opinions. Once, when he was asked to speak at the Global Dressage Forum, he declined and stated, "I only train horses as a hobby."

This hobby began many years ago when the doctor was not known except by few. In the early hours before school, Dr. Schulten-Baumer would work in the barn mucking and grooming horses. "I always liked being around horses, working with horses." Upon completing his schoolwork, the doctor would ride in the afternoons.

This schedule remained very much the same (minus the mucking) throughout the doctor's successful academic and business careers. Even after acquiring his PhD and working as a top executive in the Thyssen Corporation, Dr. Schulten-Baumer said, "I could hardly wait to come home and work with the horses. This was always the highlight of my day."

Figure 3.1

Ellen Schulten-Baumer on Donatha S, winners of the 2004 Bremen Grand Prix. They were second in 2005. Note the well-developed topline muscles and the engaged hind leg. The horse steps forward through her back and neck into a proper contact. At extended paces, the horse should seek a little more contact; at collected paces the horse should be lighter in the rider's hand. The horse's mouth is closed, indicating that the horse isn't out of balance and pulling. The slight amount of foam on the horse's lips shows proper chewing of the bit, which comes from relaxation in the back muscles.

Figure 3.2

This picture taken at the 1992 Barcelona Olympics hangs in Dr. Schulten-Baumer's barn office. Nicole Uphoff, individual and team gold medalist, worked several years with Dr. Schulten-Baumer. Isabell Werth, individual silver and team gold medalist, benefited greatly from Dr. Schulten-Baumer's instruction. (Nicole Uphoff and Isabell Werth have each won four Olympic equestrian gold medals. Monica Theodorescu, also pictured above, has won three. In the picture above, Klaus Balkenhol was the bronze medalist. The Germans placed first, second, and third—a clean sweep. The only other country to accomplish this feat was Sweden—first at the Stockholm Olympics where dressage was introduced as a sport in 1912 and again in Antwerp in 1920.)

General Questions

Why do you ride?

Riding is my passion. I love horses. I've been involved with horses as a hobby since I was a young man.

What makes a good rider?

He has to have an inborn sensibility for horses. He has to be able to feel how a horse will react. He has to be able to orientate himself to the way of the horse. He has to have good self-control. He must see the horse as a partner and not as a tool to do a sport. Of course, he must also have an inborn feel for riding. Some people don't have this. Just like some people can't get along with dogs. All of these things are necessary for a rider who wants to pursue dressage to a high level.

What makes a good trainer?

A good trainer has to be able to mentally ride along with his students. He has to know the aids and be able to talk about them. He has to not only know the reactions of the horses, he has to know in advance how the horse will react. He must master his emotions. Above all, he must see that a horse will never be pushed too hard, either physically or mentally. He has to monitor that the horse understands what the rider wants. He has to be able to explain to the rider how to get the horse to understand; otherwise there will never be an agreement or partnership. He has to be able to see if the horse is physically capable of doing what is being asked of him. The horse has to be strong enough to do the lesson. Of course the trainer has to have a good understanding of theory and of the textbooks on riding. But a good trainer has to have more. He has to be able to feel his way into the horse and rider and monitor the things that I have already mentioned. To a degree, a person has to be born with this ability.

Of course, there is much more theory that a riding teacher must master than what I have mentioned,

Figure 3.3

Dr. Schulten-Baumer concentrates on Ellen's warm-up before the Grand Prix at Bremen. The Doctor gave sporadic but accurate instructions. Every few minutes when Ellen took a break, he would give advice. He allowed the horse and rider to come together as a team with as little interference as possible. His comments enhanced the performance and kept things on the right track, but the riding lessons were done at home. "The worst show is when you feel a need to train too much in the warm-up; when you arrive and you are not properly prepared." Dr. Schulten-Baumer.

Figure 3.4
Every bit of space is utilized through careful planning. Here, the shed row stalls overlook the indoor. Shed row stalls are popular in Germany because of their superior ventilation.

and there are several books available on this theory. As a condition to my answer, I must say this because otherwise this answer is incomplete. My answer reflects some of my general thoughts on teaching, my philosophy, the how and the what of my thinking when I teach.

What physical and mental qualities are most important for a rider to develop in order to advance?

A rider has to be able to exercise self-control. He is never allowed to punish a horse unjustly, or always search for fault in the horse. He must first look for faults in himself, in his own riding or approach.

Physically, a rider has to be fit and elastic. Heavy or stiff people have a hard time riding. You can see this sometimes with older riders when they ride medium trot. If they are not elastic and athletic, the medium does not look so pleasant.

How would you define a successful day in the training of a horse?

I consider the day to be successful when the horse is happy and relaxed at the end of his work, when we have reached the level of success that we had hoped to achieve, and when we have the feeling that the horse understood what was asked of him and reacts well to the required aids.

Figure 3.5

Dr. Schulten-Baumer was one of the first to utilize the new technology of this "tidal" watering system. Underneath many types of sand, a system of pipes pumps water to and from the arena. He simply turns a dial that sets a moisture level in the footing. With one turn of his wrist he prevents both puddles and dust. The footing is a mixture of sand and shavings.

Figure 3.6

Behind this modest house in a residential neighborhood lies one of the most successful dressage barns in modern history. Most pedestrians would never know that it was there.

Figure 3.7

Dr. Schulten-Baumer started with a small 20 x 40 meter indoor riding hall. Later he added the 20 x 60 meter indoor at right angles to the existing arena. The two buildings form an "L."

When is a horse ready to advance?

Of course, the first thing that comes to mind is the scale of training: Rhythm, *losgelassenheit*, contact, impulsion, straightening, and collection. I use this scale as methodology to tell me when a horse is ready to learn. Some horses take longer to develop than others. Some are muscled very early and perform well at a young age. They are champions at the German Finals. But a horse that may be great as a Grand Prix horse does not have to perform well at a Championship for Young Horses. Many of these horses that are at the Championships [horses at the German Championships for Young Horses must qualify with a score of 8, which is comparable to an 80 percent] are not capable of performing at the advanced levels.

Do you believe that many of these young horses are pushed too hard?

Many people love it when their horse does well at the German Championships because the value of their horse rises considerably. If one is not so concerned with the value of a young horse, then these championships are not absolutely necessary.

Figure 3.8

"I believe all horses should walk a minimum of ten minutes before they begin to work. This lubricates the horse's joints and ensures that the horse begins work in a relaxed frame of mind." Dr. Schulten-Baumer.

When has a horse reached its limit?

Here we must consider the individual lessons. For example, there are many horses that have a complex about flying changes. These problems happen mostly through incorrect training. Horses develop complexes because they are afraid that they will be punished. These mental problems can be very difficult to solve.

There are also limits that are more physical in nature. Sometimes a horse will not have enough overstep in the trot; these horses will never be able do a great extension. There are also horses that have a physical problem in the walk. These physical problems can also limit a horse's potential.

When does a rider need a new horse?

Of course the possibility arises that a rider may think that he needs a new horse, but this is through

Figure 3.9

Ellen starts her pirouette at the Bremen Grand Prix. Notice the engagement of the hind legs as Donatha S lowers her croup. Ellen doesn't interfere with the pirouette by using too much leg, or worse yet, too much spur. Too much spur will cause the horse to cramp its belly muscles, thereby stopping its hind legs. As the level of engagement increases, so must the lightness of the aids. The balance and coordination between horse and rider must become more fine-tuned; this becomes easier to disturb with harsh aids. A rider must be capable of sustaining the proper level of relaxation and concentration in order to execute collected movements well. This type of focus is critical for all elite athletes—not just dressage riders. As the renowned philosopher Joseph Campbell said, "The athlete must find a place of inner peace." Note Ellen's expression.

no fault of the horse. However, I will address this question of a new dressage horse. If the horse is no longer comfortable or happy in his work, either through age, sickness, or injury, the rider should not pressure this horse to perform. If the horse can still work, but winning ribbons is impossible, the rider may want a new horse.

Did you have a favorite horse? If so, what was he like?

All horses are equally my favorite. Of course, there were horses with which I felt I shared a special relationship. One such horse was Gigolo. He could make me laugh.

How would you define excellence?

This is a difficult question...

Excellence in a dressage horse begins with conformation. This has to be exceptional. Then there has to be something inside the horse that makes him want to achieve and work. A great horse has to show himself well under a rider; his rideability must be excellent. He has to be amenable to the rider's aids. This horse has to have a happy attitude about work. These are points that I use to evaluate greatness in a horse.

If you could change one thing about the world of competitive dressage, what would it be? What is the worst thing about competitive dressage?

The worst thing is when riders push their horses too hard, when they expect more from the horse than the horse is capable of giving. This pressure can be both mental and physical. It's not so bad when I see mistakes in the lessons. This is a normal part of learning and showing.

What is the best thing about competitive dressage?

I think that dressage has a good influence on young people in particular. Dressage requires a high level of concentration. It requires an interaction with a creature, a consciousness that is much different than our own, and an acceptance of these possibilities. I believe that dressage offers good life lessons for young people. I always encouraged my children to ride dressage.

Can you describe an ideal horse show?

First it is vital that the show has good stabling and good footing so horses are not injured. The management should provide good facilities for the grooms where they can wash and shower. Good scheduling is important. A good team of judges that the riders can trust is also very essential.

Many may believe that you have always had an easy life, that you have always had great horses, that they were easy champions. But what was your greatest setback?

I did not get the most expensive horses. I searched, using my feel, to find appropriate horses for this sport, but I have had several hard setbacks. Concerning horses, I had a very nice horse that had to be put down because of a sickness. On that same day, another top horse slipped in the barn aisle and broke his leg. I lost two horses in one day.

I was about to give up this sport, but people in the Hannoveraner Verband [Hanoverian Society] persuaded me to try once more with another young horse. I went to the auction and bought another and made a new beginning.

Recently we had to put down another horse that belonged to my stepdaughter.

I have had many setbacks.

Figure 3.10
Galloping forward is important to loosen the mind and body of the dressage horse, plus it develops muscles that are necessary for piaffe and passage.

What was your greatest victory?

That is difficult to answer when I look back at my life.

It can also be more than one victory.

Well, there was the time that my son was second in the World Championships, one point out of first. Then he was second in the Alternate Olympics. Another high point was when Isabell Werth won at the European Championships. Then she won at the Olympics.

What was your most memorable ride?

My riding is not so important.

I was mostly busy as a trainer. I helped others. Of course, I won a few big Grand Prixs also, but I have enjoyed training others.

What was your worst ride?

It was painful for me at a show when I warmed up a horse too long and he couldn't perform well in the arena. I always try to not push horses too hard, or ask too much.

The best situation is when you get on a horse one half-hour before the ride. After twenty minutes, the bandages come off and you tap the groom on the shoulder and say thanks. Then you ride the test. You know it will be bad when you show up not ready, not properly prepared, and you feel like you have to train too much in the warm-up.

What do American dressage riders need to work on the most?

That is another difficult question. I am only familiar with the Americans that train over here with Klaus Balkenhol. I don't see a big difference in their riding.

Why is dressage important in the twenty-first century?

I believe that dressage is a very important sport-art. It requires a very high level of concentration and specific goals in training. It offers an opportunity for a combination of mental and physical goals to be presented at extremely high levels of achievement. This is a very significant sport-art. At least as important as running, for example, that depends solely on the individual. In dressage many factors must come together for a good performance. The horse and rider must function in harmony. The rider must be able to control his own mind and body in order to control the horse. They must function as a team in order to perform at the highest levels of competition.

TRAINING QUESTIONS

YOUNG HORSE

At what age should a horse be backed?

This answer depends on the development of the horse. One is ready a little earlier, the other a little later. Certainly it would be better to wait a little too long rather than start too early.

I'm certain that you have seen young three-year-old stallions at the test that are presented in full muscle perfection. I would rather have a horse that is four years old and has been ridden too little, rather than a horse that is three years old and has been ridden too much.

Another good advantage in a young horse is when the horse has been raised and handled well. They should be able to lead and lift their legs to have their feet cleaned. These things get more difficult as the horse gets older.

What is the most important thing when schooling a very young horse?

Again I refer to the scale of training, especially rhythm, suppleness, and impulsion. I watch that the walk stays correct, that it doesn't get hurried or hindered in any way. The walk must stay pure and completely natural.

The same goes for the trot. Of course, here we must make sure that the horse works properly in his back, that the back is not getting pushed down by the rider and that the rider is in no way interfering with the horse's natural gaits. If the rider pushes forward until the rhythm is too fast, the horse will shorten its gaits and not learn to carry with the hind legs. If the rhythm is too slow, then the horse will go into a passage-trot which causes too much tension in the back.

Figure 3.11

Ellen and Donatha S in top form at the Bremen Grand Prix. Observe the relaxation of horse and rider. As Dr. Schulten-Baumer said, "Many trainers, including many who try to copy my methods, appear to forget about the scale of training. Whenever I am experiencing a training problem with a horse, I look to the scale to see where I made a mistake." Dr. Schulten-Baumer has no wish to engage in a public debate concerning his techniques. "There are many great books on classical dressage," as he put it. He is obviously a genius for having produced so many successful Grand Prix horses. But his methods culminated into a repertoire after many years of passionate study.

Dr. Schulten-Baumer has enormous affection for his horses. He and his students are careful to not interfere with the basic rhythm of the paces. They strive to make their seat and aids work in perfect harmony with the horse. Riders should strive hard to emulate his philosophy—look to the scale of training.

Young horses must learn to lower their necks in order to strengthen their back muscles. They must become accustomed to the aids of the rider. All of these things are important in the first year of training.

What mistakes do you often observe?

I see horses getting worked too hard. I also see horses which are not learning to use their backs properly. Often these horses begin to show problems in their gaits. For example, the walk starts to have problems in the rhythm. It is possible to completely ruin a horse's walk. All of these problems can be avoided by riders who observe and adhere to the scale of training.

What should the horse know at the end of the first year of training?

This really depends on the horse and how much the back muscles have developed. A steady contact should be confirmed. The horse should be accustomed to responding to the rider's leg. The horse should be able to make transitions between the trot and the canter while maintaining its balance. These are a few of the important points.

When do you begin with lateral work?

As soon as the contact is confirmed, I begin to train leg-yielding, a good exercise to teach the horse to accept the leg and yield from it. I don't require the young horses to do a lot of steps, just a few here and there so the young horse doesn't get too stressed.

Which part of the arena do you use to train leg-yielding, the diagonal or the long side or . . . ?

As a general rule, we do not ride on the track. We ride on the inside track or even farther inside the arena so the horses learn to balance themselves, so they are not leaning on the rail.

Of course, at shows this doesn't work. We can't cause problems with the traffic, but here we train primarily on the inside track

At what age do you begin to show horses?

This is determined by the tests. Sometimes we take horses to material classes. Usually these horses are three or four years old. They are required to walk, trot, and canter around an arena in a group. As five-year-olds, the horses can begin to show a test. Usually this is the "L" level [roughly equivalent to second level in the USA].

COLLECTION

Can you describe an ideal half halt and mistakes that you often see?

We could write a book about just that. That is a difficult question. A horse accepts and allows an invisible aid to influence his stride in such a way that his legs do not track wider; he remains straight in his body. The rider should not have to pull; he should be able to maintain a normal working position. The horse's hind legs should engage more. I tell my students often, for example, when transitioning down from the extended canter, "Let the horse half halt himself." The student shouldn't pull the horse out of the extension. The student should sit in such a way that the horse accepts the half halt without pulling. Of course, this is very difficult to describe. One has to feel it. But one can also see it. You see that the horse collects out of the extension, but you don't see the rider giving an aid.

This is an example that applies to the trot as well. A rider must ride many of these invisible half halts to teach a horse to collect without losing impulsion and *losgelassenheit*. If the rider pulls too much, the horses get tight and resistant. The rider must gradually train the horse's response to the half halt. You can't expect the response all at once.

Do you use one form of lateral work more often than the others?

Yes, I use shoulder-in the most.

Figure 3.12

From this angle it is easiest to observe that the horse is stepping forward and through with all four legs. This is an important aspect of the shoulder-in that is often ignored by many riders. In order to maintain the rhythm and *losgelassenheit* of the gait, the rider must drive forward and refrain from using too much hand, especially too much inside rein.

Figure 3.13

From these pictures it is easy to see that the horse is properly bent and stepping forward. The mouth of the horse is closed and the slight foam on the horse's lips indicates chewing and a soft contact with the rider's hands. An open mouth or the tongue drawn up or, worse yet, the tongue sticking out, are signs of fundamental problems in the scale of training.

Figure 3.14

Note the consistency of the bend and expression in the trot and the relaxation in the horse and rider.

Figure 3.15

Whereas many Grand Prix riders have trouble training a second horse to the highest levels of competition, Ellen's concentration and consistency of performance, under the guidance of Dr. Schulten-Baumer, enabled her to train her current five Grand Prix horses. Of course, a surprising number Grand Prix riders skip the training process entirely; they purchase made, successful horses.

Figure 3.16
Again it is easy to see that the horse is stepping forward and sideways in the lateral work. The horse covers ground in a rhythmic, springy manner. A soft inside rein allows for good shoulder freedom and expression.

Figure 3.17
The rider sits more on the inside seat bone, over the weight-carrying leg. Ellen's inside leg is forward and her outside leg is back, which helps the horse to bend throughout its entire body. This facilitates the reaching and crossing of the horse's legs.

Figure 3.18
Horses that are not capable of sustaining a nice bend throughout their entire body, without too much inside rein, are not ready to half pass. "Training at home is done primarily without whips. In general, the more that whips are used, the worse the result," says Dr. Schulten-Baumer.

Which combinations of lateral work do you prefer?

I use shoulder-in to half pass, or *volte* to half pass.

What are common mistakes in the lateral work?

One of the most common mistakes that I see is that in the shoulder-in the horse slips out with his outside shoulder. In other words, the horse bends his neck but doesn't step onto three tracks with his legs and bring his shoulders in. The half halt and the aids

Figure 3.19

"I learned something very important from my father," Ellen Schulten-Baumer said. "When a horse doesn't perform a lesson as expected, I first have to ask myself if the horse is capable. If the answer is yes, then I must think about how I apply my aids. I must use them better so the horse understands exactly what I want. This may involve riding more preparatory exercises. If I can't get it right fairly quickly, then I go to something else. It is unfair and unproductive to drill a horse; this causes too much physical and mental stress. I tell my students this also. If they just can't get it right, they can think about their aids overnight and try again tomorrow. Then the horse and rider get a fresh start together."

don't go through the horse's body; the horse brings his neck in but not the shoulders. I see this mistake very often.

When is a horse ready to collect?

As soon as the horse is steady in the contact and begins to accept half halts, he begins to collect.

When do you begin to train flying changes?

We have had talented young horses that offered flying changes. We accepted the offers. In these circumstances, we train flying changes even before we train counter canter. In general, if you train too much counter canter so the counter canter gets stabilized, it gets harder to train changes. This can be a problem for horses that show a lot at the "L" level, where counter canter is required.

How do you usually train changes? Which figures and lines do you use?

I prefer to train flying changes on straight lines. Some people train changes in the corners. I'm not a fan of that technique. For horses that have problems, I use curved lines. I try to vary the spot where I ask

Figure 3.20

Ellen trains the piaffe on Donatha S. Note the uphill frame and the engagement of the hindquarters. Ellen sits quietly without interfering with the motion of the horse. This enables the horse to maintain sufficient *losgelassenheit* for this most difficult exercise.

for the change. If the horse always changes in the same spot, he anticipates, gets tense, and makes a mistake. In this case simply ask for the change on a different spot. The horse must stay *losgelassen* with plenty of impulsion for the change to be correct.

Learning the flying change is a very important step in the development of the horse. Under no circumstances should a rider punish a horse that makes a mistake. This leads to tension that causes a horse to have problems with changes. They develop a complex.

When is a horse ready to learn piaffe and how do you train this exercise?

My approach differs according to the talent of the horse and the ability of the rider. We train some horses on the double longe and carefully encourage forward from behind. It is then very important to see exactly the moment when the horse begins to understand the direction of the training. At that point we reward him with pats or some sugar. This makes a strong impression in the horse's mind, and he begins to understand what the rider wants. When you have reached this point, where the horse begins to understand half steps, you have made significant progress.

At what age do you usually begin to train piaffe?

I don't have a specific age requirement for this lesson. Of course, the horse has to be confirmed on the aids and good in the contact. But I see nothing wrong with asking a horse to take two or three half steps either under saddle or on the double longe. In some ways it is easier on the double longe because the horse has an easier time using his back properly and keeping his balance.

I have a young horse now that was somewhat on the aids when he came. I didn't think that he could learn piaffe yet, because he didn't seem to have the ability. We taught him to lower his neck and relax his back. He began to chew the bit with a closed mouth. We worked him very quietly.

One day I started quietly encouraging him to take a couple half steps, but I really didn't think he would learn this. I then trained the half steps a little bit every day, just enough so he wouldn't get tense. Many days later, to my complete surprise, he began a beautiful piaffe. He understood. I rewarded him immediately.

Another horse that came to this farm had developed problems with the piaffe. If he just thought about piaffe, he would get very tense. He would go crazy. We solved this by riding trot-halt transitions. As the rider was trotting into the halt, she would think about piaffe for a couple of steps and then halt. It was important not to ask for too much, just a couple of steps and then halt so that the horse learned not to be afraid. When this horse understood the piaffe, he also understood how to do terrific transitions between the piaffe and passage. This horse became a champion.

There are many different approaches when training horses. If one approach doesn't work, then you must think of a different way, a different method. You must always think and try different things. There are lots of roads.

Do you teach piaffe or passage first?

Usually I train piaffe first. If a horse has learned to passage first, piaffe can be difficult to learn. The horse always tries to go into the passage rhythm when he should piaffe.

What are some common mistakes?

Well . . . horses get cramped and tight. When this happens, they lose their ability to pick up their feet. Horses must maintain *losgelassenheit* in the piaffe. They must understand the lesson. Also, some horses do not piaffe on the spot, they piaffe going forward. This is a common mistake. Some horses are not even behind; they lift one leg more than the other. This comes from the riding and training or the rider gave uneven aids.

Of course, some horses are more talented than others for these lessons. One must always try to achieve good *durchlässigkeit*[15] [through-allowing-ness] then you can see if the horse has talent or not. Many times the problems in the advanced lessons come from lack of training in the basics. When you run into problems, you have to try a different approach; an approach that includes training in *losgelassenheit* and *durchlässigkeit*.

---

[15] *Durchlässigkeit* is usually translated as responsiveness. It occurs when a horse allows an aid to go through its body; for example, when a half halt goes through the entire topline to the hindquarters, or a driving aid elicits an immediate, but rhythmic, response forward. *Durchlässigkeit* only happens after the rider has achieves sufficient *losgelassenheit*. *Durchlässigkeit*, like *losgelassenheit*, cannot be forced into the horse. They must be developed by careful, sensitive riding.

Figure 3.21

This well-developed horse shows engagement and carrying power as she starts her pirouette.

Figure 3.22

Note the considerable engagement even as the horse has entered the downward phase of the canter stride.

Figure 3.23

How do you train pirouettes?

My approach differs. We have a horse now that we train from the half pass. We ride a half pass, then collect the horse more and introduce the pirouette. This worked well for this horse.

I also start by cantering on a big circle, then slowly decreasing the size of the circle. The horse must keep jumping forward in an even canter rhythm.

Some horses learn by shortening the canter on a straight line and starting the pirouette.

What are some common mistakes?

There are a lot of mistakes: The horse canters parallel [hind feet and front feet stay together]. The horse falls out behind [the pirouette is not small enough]. The horse throws himself around the circle; he doesn't stay on the aids. The horse slows the canter too much and gets behind the rider's aids. The horse doesn't stay in balance. The horse gets too deep in front. These are a few of the common mistakes.

In general I find it important see each horse as an individual, to watch each horse's reactions. They all react somewhat differently. The goals of the German training system and those of the FEI are good, but out of necessity they are very general. Here we contemplate each horse as an individual, and we always think of slightly different approaches so the horse understands what we want. Yesterday we had a horse responding poorly in his training, so I asked myself, "What mistakes have I made? Where did I drift off of the correct path?" I always go back to the scale of training. First and foremost the rhythm has to be there. If the rhythm is wrong, it is like trying to drive a car with a flat tire. If the rhythm is wrong, then you must find out why. Often, horses with rhythm faults are lacking in *losgelassenheit* [loose/supple-allowingness[16]]. And so, you begin to solve the puzzle.

---

[16] Again the key word here is *allowing*. The horse has to understand what you want, then he will allow this supple, loose way of going into his motion. This cannot be forced. It must be developed.

CHAPTER FOUR

GEORGE THEODORESCU

Brief Bio

George Theodorescu, a native of Romania, moved to Germany at age thirty-one as a political refugee. He found success and friendship in his new home, where he rapidly rose to the status of elite trainer after numerous victories in international competition. His daughter, Monica, has been riding in top international competitions since she was in her teens. She has won three Olympic gold medals as a part of the German dressage team, was three times a World Cup champion, a bronze medalist at the WEG in Stockholm, and the winner of many other international medals and competitions. His wife Inge, a Grand Prix jumper and Grand Prix dressage rider, has won the Hamburg Ladies Dressage Derby four years running and has trained the Polish dressage team.

Many nations have benefited from the classical knowledge of Theodorescu. He has coached the French, Italian, Russian, and USA dressage squads, as well as individual riders representing many countries of the world. He also speaks five languages fluently, and his love for music, ballet, and the arts come close to matching his love for horses.

Figure 4.1

General Questions

Why do you ride?

Riding is passion number one for me.

What makes a good rider?

A good rider needs a lot of patience. You must treat a horse like a child, like your own child. You have to raise them with kindness and understanding. You must take the time to show them how to do things right. Horses are remarkably willing when they understand exactly what you expect from them. If the rider confuses the horse with sloppy or inaccurate aids, the horse shouldn't be blamed or punished for not understanding. Riders who feel that they must constantly correct their horses need to focus more attention on their own aids; they are not being clear. A good rider recognizes this and always tries to ride well and without interfering with the natural gaits of the horse. He rewards the horse for each step of progress. In this way the rider instills a work ethic and discipline into the horse without using violence.

A rider must have an understanding of a horse's balance and center of gravity. A horse is standing on four legs, a rider on two. A horse's balance is completely different. When a rider sits on a horse, the rider must learn to think like a horse, not like a pedestrian.

A soldier can turn on a dime. A horse, with his four legs, turns on a completely different radius. A rider must always take this into consideration. He must learn to think like a horse. He must learn to take the horse's center of gravity into consideration with every turn or movement he rides. A rider must never disturb a horse's center of gravity.

I am a skier. When I skied as a young man, I often wore a backpack. This had to be fitted very well and snugly, otherwise it would cause me to fall down. A rider must think the same way about his seat in every lesson that he rides. That means in walk, trot, and canter, or while jumping or racing, the rider must always follow the horse's motion. This is often the source of many problems. Often, riders interfere with the natural gaits of the horse. It is the rider's job to understand this, not the horse's job. The rider should never expect the horse to change himself to fit the rider, to change his movement or his thinking to that of a pedestrian. This is very important and not as obvious as it seems.

Horses are humanity's best friends. They have done everything for us, their friends. Think about war. Think about bad weather. Think about the Wild West in America. What would they have done without the horse? In many states there are still laws on the books which allow capital punishment for a horse thief. If you catch somebody stealing your horse, you can shoot them out of the saddle. These laws came about because people needed their horses. One hundred sixty years ago, they didn't even have a bicycle for transportation. Sure, people can fly to the moon today, but in our recent history we depended upon the horse. Can you imagine a journey of 1,600 or 1,800 miles without a horse? Most people wouldn't survive these trips. That's why people were allowed to shoot horse thieves. Horses were cherished because the horse was always there for us.

This is how I came to the conclusion that if a horse can, he will. In other words, if horses are mentally and physically able to perform a task, they will complete this duty for us; but they have to know how first. If we now think about this theme, we arrive at a better understanding of dressage.

Dressage is made up of a series of movements and exercises. These exercises should become a dance between rider and horse. A dance cannot be forced. Draw reins are often used to force horses into submission—and the whip. Imagine if somebody tied me up, hit me with a whip, and said dance. The result

Figure 4.2

Monica Theodorescu communicates with her seven-year-old mount Whisper prior to a demonstration ride at the 2005 German Championships for Young Horses. Monica and George Theodorescu don't believe that young horse classes are necessary in training a horse for upper levels of competition. Whisper competed in his fifth show at Aachen in the Prix St. Georges and was third. "Too often, riders will stress their mounts for young horse classes (four-year-old classes). Theodorescu believes many riders focus too much on winning. As opposed to being a healthy learning experience for a young equine, these classes can teach an overly worked horse to hide his talents instead of showing off. Riders should make these classes a fun learning experience for the horse, and then there are fewer problems later."

would not be a dance. I might want to kill this person, but the beauty of the dance would be lost.

Or, what if a person brought me to a heavy object and said that I should lift this thing and I was not able? What if he then beat me and I still couldn't lift the object? He could beat me all day and night, and it wouldn't help because I simply lacked the ability. This would be bad enough if it only happened once. I could recover if this barbarian never returned, but what if it happened every day, around the same time and at the same place? What if he showed up with his weight and a club? After one week I wouldn't sleep anymore. I wouldn't eat any more.

And this is supposed to be a dance???

A horse would look at this person and think, "There is the one that beats me and works me too hard." He would not want to be a dance partner.

In contrast to this, I attended a ballet as a child where a ballerina stood on her toes and smiled. She had to train for many years to do this, but she made it look easy. This image has always stayed with me.

In more recent times, I saw a ballerina of the Bolshoi Ballet perform in London. After an incredible performance, she came back onto the stage, stood on her toe, and performed thirty pirouettes. The audience was going mad. They applauded and screamed out loud the number of each pirouette. When she finished, she got a standing ovation. She merely bowed her head to the audience and humbly accepted their praise. She left the stage, then returned and did thirty pirouettes on the other foot. Now the audience went really wild. They stood on their chairs and clapped. The ballerina again bowed her head slightly and humbly accepted their applause.

When I apply this to dressage and to training horses, I think of the center line and moments after the final salute. When I see a competitor raise their fist and swing their arm through the air in self-congratulatory elation, I am reminded of the humble ballerina, a person dedicated to her art and dedicated to ever greater levels of perfection. An artist with this demeanor would also be able to learn the art of training horses.

Dressage is not just a sport. Yes, a part of it is about competing and trying to come in first. But dressage is only beautiful when it is done well, when the rider and horse dance in harmony. If a rider has not reached that stage with his horse, he should stay home. He should not perform in public.

Dressage also has to be fun for the horse. When you see a horse on the pasture and he gets excited, he begins to passage. He is saying, "Look at me. Look at this." This is why I don't understand some of these training methods, like draw reins. If you think about dressage and the theory behind it, the horse has to get lower behind, not in front. The horse has to take more weight onto his hindquarters.

A good rider must have a passion for horses. This will help him to learn how horses think so he can have a better relationship with the horse. He will have an easier time understanding some of these points.

What makes a good trainer?

A very important quality would again be patience. A trainer has to deal with two beginners. Of course, this means there will be a lot of difficulties. One of the biggest problems is that these students have different centers of gravity. The trainer must understand this and communicate it to the student.

Horses are born with more weight on the forehand. The weight of the rider gets added to this. All of this extra weight that is on the forehand has to be sent back to the haunches. But this process takes time. The horse has to be made strong first. Young horses want to please, to do things right, but they are not able. They must have the ability first. This is logic.

The horse must be ridden forward in an even rhythm. This builds sufficient muscles to carry this weight. If a rider tries to force this process too fast, he can injure the horse, both in the mind and the body. Such a rider, who forces things too fast, is not a friend of the horse. As a friend, he should make sure that his horse is also having fun, just like the horse on the pasture.

In order to take the weight on the haunches, a horse has to learn to lower his croup. When he lowers his croup, he raises his withers. When the withers come up, so does the horse's head and neck. Only through this process does a horse come into balance with a rider. When this is done properly, the horse maintains a beautifully even and regular rhythm in all gaits. The walk and canter remain pure. The trot keeps good *losgelassenheit* and impulsion.

A trainer has to learn to understand the nature and the mind of the horse. Some people think that horses are dumb. Horses are often much faster in

Figure 4.3

George Theodorescu focuses his intense concentration on Aleksandra Korelov, who rides the stallion Balagur for Russia. When Mr. Theodorescu first saw Balagur, the stallion worked as a police horse in a small Siberian town located well to the north of Moscow. "I was told he would stand all day through any kind of weather that Siberia could throw his way. He was particularly good at rowdy soccer games. I replied that I needed him to move and not just stand. They told me he had a very good flying change, and they sent me a video. When I saw the video, he changed from right to left but not from left to right. But there was something that I liked about him—a certain carriage that demonstrated his intelligence. He learned everything in a Grand Prix very quickly. He performed well at Aachen and the European Championships less than a year and a half after starting dressage training."

their heads than humans. For example, a rider will take his horse on a trail ride, and the horse will suddenly become nervous and stop. The rider thinks, "What's wrong with him, what's upsetting him?" Behind a meadow are two deer that the horse noticed right away, but the somewhat thick rider is still asking, "What is wrong?"

A horse has to be a friend to the rider, as an equal, just like a human. The trainer can't think of the animal as a dumb beast. Animals are very clever. We have a tree where a pair of birds nest every year. Every spring they return to the same tree after flying thousands of kilometers. They don't have a GPS, a cell phone, or a compass, but every year they find the same spot. This cannot be considered dumb.

A trainer has to be observant. He has to watch the horses and figure out what they are thinking. This requires a feel for horses. This feel is directly connected

Figures 4.4–4.5

Although the two pictures above and the one on page 115 were taken from slightly different angles, the pictures clearly demonstrate that Monica Theodorescu has mastered keeping a majority of her weight over her inside seat bone in the half pass. During this demonstration ride at the 2005 Global Dressage Forum on seven-year-old Whisper, Monica has clearly placed more of her weight to the inside and turned her inside shoulder back. Her outside leg is behind the girth, and her inside leg is on the girth—in each half pass, left and right. It can be a very surprising exercise to look at pictures of dressage riders—even those taken of top riders—and see how many of them are sitting with more of their weight over the wrong seat bone, the outside seat bone. It seems that a slight majority of riders keep more of their weight over their right seat bone in both directions—even in the left half pass. This could be because of right-side dominance in most riders; people have more trouble controlling the left sides of their bodies. As George Theodorescu says, "When the rider has more of his weight over the outside seat bone, it makes the job of the horse much more difficult. More of the rider's weight should be over the inside, weight-carrying hind leg."

---

to passion. There is a relationship between passion and feel, just as there is between respect and friendship. A rider that uses his horse like a tool has no respect for horses and no love. He is not a friend of the horse. This rider will never learn to dance with horses.

A trainer has to develop an eye for a horse's capabilities. Someone could beat me all night, and I would not be able to sing like Pavarotti. Not every horse can jump two meters. Not every horse can be a race horse. A trainer has to have an understanding of these things.

What physical and mental qualities are most important for a rider to develop in order to advance?

A rider must have a deep passion for the horse. If he has that, it's enough.

How would you define a successful day of training?

Mostly, you can see this on a daily basis. It is important not to ask for the horse to progress too much in

Figure 4.6
Again we see a consistency of performance in this three-time Olympic gold medalist. The relaxation and focus in the horse come from the relaxation and focus in the rider. Top athletes learn to perform from a place of inner tranquility. In order to epitomize this degree of focus, the rider must practice this concentration on a daily basis—until a rider can ride each corner correctly and stay relaxed. The little pieces are important. The horse will then learn relaxation from the rider. An anxious, domineering rider will cause tension in the horse—this pair will resonate tension. This angst will be most evident for untrained eyes at the walk and the halt.

one day. Then you notice that next week the horse moves better than the week before. The horse has to feel good and be happy in his work. Sometimes you run into barriers in the daily work. But you have to analyze and figure out why you encountered this barrier. There must be a reason, a problem with the training, with the rider's approach. You have to also keep in mind that some horses are more talented than others so you don't push a horse past his natural abilities, but horses will always try once they understand what you want. I've never encountered a horse that just didn't want to learn anything at all.

When is a horse ready to advance?

A rider can never think of teaching a horse a new lesson all at once in any complete form. There are many exercises that prepare each lesson. These exercises are not only important for the horse, but for the rider as well. If the rider doesn't get the horse to successfully learn the new lesson, then the rider doesn't learn it either. They must learn as a team. The rider can give the wrong aids or sit wrong in the saddle, and he will get the wrong result.

Let's take a simple lesson as an example, a transition to canter. This simple lesson leads to more difficult lessons like the pirouettes and flying changes. Transitions within the canter also help horses learn these more difficult lessons. But we have to start this learning process with the transition to canter.

There are discussions about the aids even for this simple exercise. Most books in Germany say the rider should sit with more weight on the inside seat bone. This is a mistake. I'm not sure where it originated, but once this mistake started to be printed, everybody kept repeating it. One book says to sit more on the outside seat bone. This is the book that first discusses the importance of a rider transferring most of his weight to one seat bone, and the book that everybody incorrectly quotes from, including the German Training Manuals. Steinbrecht, the famous trainer and author, claimed in his book *The Gymnasium of the Horse* that riders should sit on the outside seat bone when asking for the canter.

It doesn't matter what a person claims; one must be able to prove his claims with logic and reason. I believe that Steinbrecht was right. He claimed that since the transition to canter leads to the flying change, a rider should sit with more weight on the same seat bone as in the flying change. If I want to ride a flying change from the right canter to the left, then I would put more weight on the right seat bone. As proof of his logic, Steinbrecht said a rider should never place more of his weight over the hind leg that is farthest from the horse's center of gravity. The rider's weight would interfere and cause the horse to work harder with this leg.

For example, in the left canter, the horse's right hind leg is farther back, and the left hind leg is farther forward, so as the horse canters, I would sit more to the left. The left hind carries more weight, because it steps under closer to the horse's center of gravity. The right hind pushes more. If I wanted to ride a flying change from left to right, I should sit more on the left during the change because the horse's right hind leg must achieve the greatest distance of stride. If my weight were more on the right, I would interfere and make his job harder. The transition to canter should be ridden the same as the flying change, with more of the rider's weight on the outside. In the canter one hind leg is already under the horse, and the other is farther behind. By keeping my weight over the hind leg that is already under the horse during the flying change, the horse can jump with more elevation of the new inside hind leg. This leg travels the greater distance to step under the horse.[17]

This is a very logical argument for Steinbrecht's claim. It is hard to dispute. Much of riding is like mathematics. One and one is two. One and one is never one and three-fourths. And so, when a rider teaches a new lesson to a horse, the rider must always consider how the horse moves with his four legs. He must always make sure that the horse understands the preparatory exercises. Then he must introduce these new lessons in a way that does not interfere with the horse's natural gaits. He must be patient as the horse learns and makes mistakes. He must not drill the horse endlessly, and he must always reward the horse when he gets it right.

I believe the mistake about the weight being more on the inside seat bone for the canter departure came from riding remounts, the horses that are newly under saddle. These horses know nothing about a rider's aids and how to move off of the leg. To canter these horses, a rider accelerates the trot in a corner or on a circle. The young horse loses his balance and falls into the canter. These young horses learn best when the rider sits more on the inside seat bone so they fall into the canter in the right direction and take the correct lead.

With more advanced horses that understand the leg, and particularly with horses that are doing flying changes, pirouettes, and half pass, a rider must always consider how he will cause the least amount of interference with the horse's four legs. He must always keep more of his weight over the leg that is most under the

---
[17] This is a very interesting concept that changes many conceptions about a rider's weight aids. Many riders believe that if they press down on the inside seat bone, it will cause the horse to bend. But this act of pressing down could cause the rider to stiffen and interfere with the horse's motion. As opposed to this, a rider who thinks about lightening the outside seat bone in order to not interfere with the horse's natural gaits will be less inclined to get stiff and against the motion of the horse.

Figure 4.7

A horse's center of gravity is below and just behind the withers, roughly in the middle of a horse's body. In the left canter, Monica Theodorescu sits with more of her weight over the carrying inside hind leg since this leg is closest to the horse's center of gravity. The pushing outside hind leg has the farthest distance to travel to come under the horse's center of gravity. A rider should always sit with more weight over the carrying leg to make the horse's job easier. Think of holding a bucket of water with your arm next to your body, close to your center of gravity. Now picture holding a bucket of water with your arm extended away from your center of gravity. The farther your arm is away from your center, the harder your job.

Figure 4.8

Monica rides the canter half pass in the warm-up arena. Monica weights her left seat bone and rides the horse uphill with the poll at the highest point. The horse travels in self-carriage; she uses her aids only to make a change. Note that in this series of pictures that continues on the next page, Monica blinks in the rhythm of the half pass.

Figure 4.9

Notice that the horse steps forward and sideways; the canter stride doesn't shorten significantly for the lateral movement.

horse. In this way a rider strives to lighten the load of the horse. A rider must learn to think like a horse. He must always take four legs into consideration.

This principle holds especially true in the half pass. Riders often sit on the wrong side of the horse's back. The outside leg, the pushing leg, has the longest distance to travel, so the rider must be careful to not burden this leg with too much weight. The rider must sit with more weight on the inside seat bone, over the carrying leg. This helps the horse to step shorter with the inside hind leg so the outside hind has an easier time reaching forward and crossing over. Dressage should be a dance. The rider must always take care to not interfere with the horse's natural gaits. He must make the horse's job easier. The horse's legs should spring lightly from the ground in the half pass.

When has a horse reached its limit?

It is very difficult to define this limit. On the other hand, it is very easy to say, "That horse will never learn. He will never be anything." I haven't had many horses that couldn't learn. I had heard from others that they couldn't learn or that they didn't want to

Figures 4.10–4.13

Too often riders will continually spur a horse to move sideways. This causes the horse to constrict in his side and interferes with the horse's ability to move. Once again, a rider who uses too much of an aid will find that aid ineffective. He will be tempted to use more; thus, he perpetuates a bad cycle. The horse will not dance.

Figure 4.14
The indoor arena at George Theodorescu's farm. The kick boards are high enough so the horses will not be startled or distracted by a partially hidden object that suddenly pops into view. The windows allow plenty of natural light. An overhead watering system prevents dust and helps bind the footing, a sand and shavings mixture.

learn, or that a horse would never amount to anything, but these situations developed in a very positive way for the horses once they were here; they learned anyway. As I mentioned before, the horse and rider must have a good relationship, a friendship. This helps in the learning process. Then there are thousands and thousands of small pieces that make a difference. Sometimes these small pieces turn into very big ones over time; they play a very big role. Of course, some horses will never learn to perform as well as others. Some horses have more ability than others. But to say that a horse can't learn anything is absolute nonsense. They can all learn.

When does a rider need a new horse?

He needs a new horse when his old horse is too old. Maybe you noticed these horses in the paddocks. One is Ganimedes and the other is Grunox. Both of them went to the Olympics and won team gold medals. They stay outside most of the day when the weather permits. We just lost one at the age of thirty-two. We got him as a three-year-old. Monica rode him in the Young Rider Division. Then they went to the World Cup.

They stand out there and eat grass, but sometimes they watch the other horses perform in the dressage arena. They remember those days well.

Figure 4.15
Shed row stalls around a courtyard form an attractive entrance to Gestüt Lindenhof, home of the Theodorescus. These stalls provide superior ventilation for horses.

How do you define a great horse?

Each horse is great in his own way.

Did you have a favorite horse?

All of them.

What is excellence?

Excellence is a superlative. Excellence would be somewhat more common, but most people don't want to work to achieve it. Many talented singers will contemplate and practice a difficult opera for hours each day to achieve a level of excellence. When talent and practice unite, you achieve excellence. It is a form of brilliance that is uncommon.

If you could change one thing about the world of competitive dressage, what would it be?

Many years ago in Germany, we had a system of judging our national classes where the judges sat together and discussed the ride as it happened. There were certain protocols. At the end, the judges gave one score for the ride instead of each giving an

Figure 4.16

Above, Monica Theodorescu rides Whisper at the 2005 Global Dressage Forum. She demonstrates how this seven-year-old is learning to piaffe. She is careful not to ask for too many steps or the horse will get too tense. Excessive tension would cause the horse to lose the *losgelassenheit* in its back, and the horse would no longer be able to move its legs in even diagonal pairs; the steps of the hind and front legs would be disconnected. Only through careful, educated training can horses such as Whisper be brought to the highest levels. The rider must always be careful not to interfere with the natural gaits of the horse. When *losgelassenheit* suffers, regularity of the gaits suffers as well.

individual score. They also gave some advice to the rider about what should be done with the horse to improve the performance.

I believe that in order to bring the judges together to discuss dressage it wouldn't be wrong to reintroduce this system of judging. The judges could discuss and learn from each other as the test was happening. Perhaps every class shouldn't be judged this way, but some, including those at an international level, should be judged like this.

Currently we have judges arriving at a show from many countries. The judge from Canada might have one rider placed first. The judge from Mexico and the one from Germany might place different riders first. If the judges discussed their results and then agreed upon a winner, then we would have only one winner. This would also provide judges with less experience a chance to educate their eyes.

It doesn't make any sense to curse the judges for doing a poor job. The judges are trying to do their best. But if they had a chance to ask a question during a test, if they had a chance to discuss movements, then we might eliminate the scenario where one judge places a rider first and another places him last. The judges do not like it when this happens either, but they must function within the system that we have built for them.

For the riders and the sport, this system would have immediate benefits. The rider would receive combined critique and one score. If one judge gives him a 6 and another a 5, he receives a 5.5. In his critique he hears, "If you improve in these areas, your score will be better." The improvement could take place from one day to the next. The rider would know exactly in which areas he must improve instead of receiving several differing opinions of his work. There would be much less confusion. Of course, we could still judge some classes the way we do now, but introducing this old system in some of the classes would have many benefits.

Figure 4.17
Monica Theodorescu displays classic form in this turn. The harmony and relaxation of horse and rider are clearly evident. She has her inside leg forward, her outside leg back. This helps the horse to bend through the length of his body. Monica's weight is over the inside hind, the weight carrying leg, which steps shorter. This doesn't interfere with the pushing leg, the outside hind, which has the longer distance to travel to reach under the horse's center of gravity. The horse travels with his poll at the highest point with an elastic, light contact.

What is the best thing about competitive dressage?

Why does a singer stand on a stage and sing, or why does somebody else play an instrument? A violinist enters a concert hall and plays a concerto . . . why? If he stayed at home, nobody would say anything—good or bad. A jumper rider chooses to jump a course. Another rider may choose to hack in the woods. Nobody is forced to do anything that they don't like. A show is

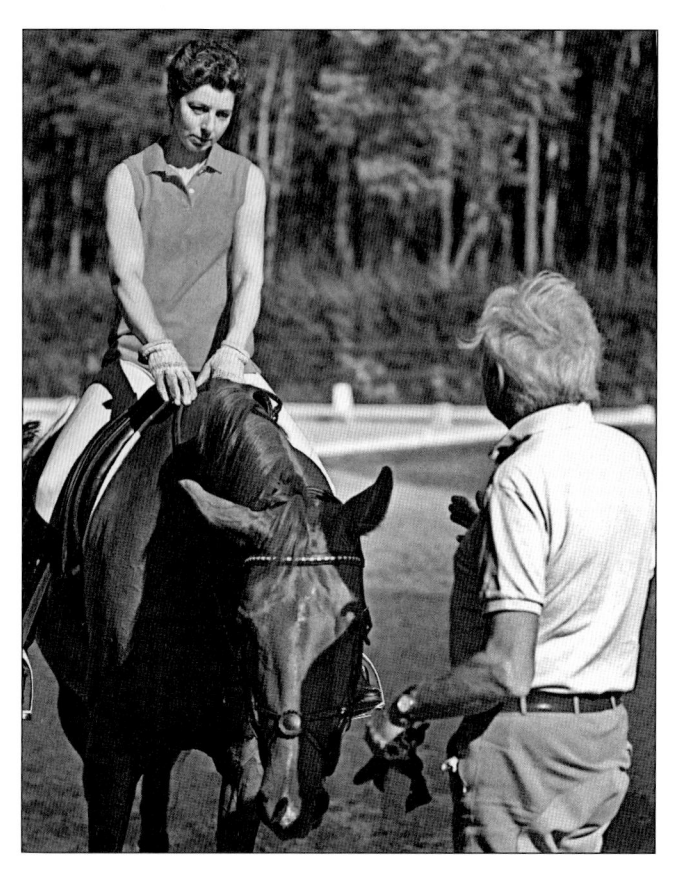

Figure 4.18
Monica listens intently to advice from her father and mentor. Even after numerous championship titles in major international competitions, Monica Theodorescu obviously receives instruction eagerly. Elite athletes from all sports need a coach. The best riders seek the dressage masters.

a place to present one's talent, a place where one can try to achieve excellence.

Can you describe an ideal horse show?

An ideal show should be a festival with people and horses. It should reflect the passions of the people involved with horses.

What was your greatest victory?

My biggest victory was my daughter.

What was your worst ride?

When I was not in form and I didn't ride well enough, when my riding didn't do the horse justice.

Can you share a humorous experience with us?

I am fortunate because I have had many funny experiences in my life. The one that comes to mind now is something that happened one year at the Bremen show. This was a prestigious show where the best riders competed, many of them Olympic medalists. There was a tradition there for a pair's class which was ridden to music on one of the days of competition. Over the years I had several partners in this class. I rode together with my wife [champion Grand Prix jumper and dressage rider], and Gabriella Grillo [Olympic team gold medalist], and my daughter [six-time Olympic team gold medalist]. We always won.

One year my wife and I were invited to compete, but we were very busy before the show. We didn't figure out our choreography or music. We kept saying, "We'll do it. We'll do it." But we never got around to it.

The night before our class we were invited to a party with many of our good friends. One dance led to another, the next story had to be told, and we had one more glass of wine. Before we knew it, it was five in the morning.

Luckily, we were scheduled to ride last in the class. I told my wife that I would go into the riding hall and talk to the man in charge of the music. I knew him. I hoped he would help us out.

I'll never forget. There was this small iron ladder that rose to a small room at the top of the very high indoor ceiling of the sports stadium. In my wobbly riding boots, I climbed the long ladder. At the top, when I opened the door, I saw a man who looked like he was in worse shape than me. We laughed at the sight of each other. I told him my problem. I asked him to play a waltz for the canter, something slower for the piaffe and passage. He asked me what I wanted exactly, and I told him that I had to warm up my horse. Could he please improvise?

My wife and I warmed up our horses. She came to me and asked, "What do we do now?" It was time to enter the arena.

I replied, "We'll enter in the passage, and then we'll talk about it."

We entered and I said under my breath, "You go left and I'll go right." We made it through the class in this manner. Half pass, extended trot, we talked about it in the corners. "Let's piaffe here, and then we'll passage, canter forward and ride a pirouette."

My guess is that our horses really helped us to put on a good performance. The judges must have been watching their brilliance more than our mistakes. They seemed to have lots of energy, which helped compensate for our lack of planning. When the results were tallied, our horses won the class. The partnership between horse and rider is not always fifty/fifty.

What advice can you give to an aspiring rider?

I spoke once with Hans Guenther Winkler about this subject. He said it best. The young people who are coming up in the sport have to burn with desire to learn. When I think about the time when I started into this sport, I was always thinking about the barn and horses. I never needed an alarm clock. I still don't own an alarm clock. I wake up early no matter how late I go to bed. Even when I was a kid, I woke up early because I wanted to go to the barn and see the horses.

Why is dressage important in the twenty-first century?

We talked about the importance of horses to humanity at the beginning of the interview. Maybe we don't need horses for transportation anymore, but it is a part of our culture, even our ancient culture, to have an interest in horses. Without horses we wouldn't be here having this conversation. Without horses there would not be sports as we know them today or an Olympics.

Dressage is an Olympic discipline. Many people like to come and watch the horses perform. We are better for having been around horses. Horses need to be trained and educated. We had a horse that was thirty-two years old on our pasture. He had a good life. Dressage was good for him. We owe horses a lot. Why should we punish them now by not having a job for them, a use for them?

The public has proven that they like to watch horse sports. We have to watch more than just airplanes and 300 horsepower cars. They crash now and then anyway. We watch people run, whether it's 100 meters or a 5K. We watch because there is a connection with the athlete, with his training and discipline. The connection with the horse and rider is greater because we also connect with our history and pay homage to a valued friend. Do you really think that there are people who don't want to watch horses? I don't think so.

What else you would like to share with the dressage world?

Recently I gave a clinic where one of the world's top Grand Prix riders suggested to me that they take the walk work out of the Grand Prix. He claimed that walking was boring for the spectators. We should eliminate the walk and perhaps add more piaffe and passage.

Dressage is founded upon the rhythm and purity of the gaits, the walk, trot, and canter. Once again, this concept is more profound than it seems. The wisdom that the masters of this sport developed over the ages is truly astounding. If a young horse is pushed too hard, if a rider tries to change the balance of the horse too fast by engaging the hindquarters before the

Figure 4.19

This horse displays the type of dissociation normally associated with a traditional four-beat canter. The horse is in the counter canter. His left hind has already struck the ground. The diagonal pair, the right hind and left front, shows clear negative dissociation. The left front will hit the ground prior to the right hind. The horse's left legs will hit the ground first, followed by his right legs—a lateral canter.

Figure 4.20

The horse continues in his canter. The left legs have already touched down. The right hind closely followed the left front.

Figures 4.19–4.24

Although George Theodorescu had nothing to do with the training of the horse in this series of pictures, taken at the World Championships for Young Horses, they help illustrate his point about the deterioration of the walk affecting the purity of the canter. When a horse develops a lateral walk, the right legs move forward together with little or no separation (right-hind right-front), and the left legs move forward together with little or no separation (left-hind left-front). The masters throughout many centuries of training dressage horses noticed a correlation between a lateral walk and a lateral canter. It seems when a horse develops a lateral walk, this tendency of moving laterally somehow is transferred to the canter. Note in the pictures, the horse's left legs hit the ground first, followed by the right legs. This depicts the traditional four-beat canter, which shows a negative dissociation[18] of the diagonal pair; it is nearly a lateral gait.

Figure 4.21
The last leg to touch down is the right front.

Figure 4.22
The inside front is the last leg to lift prior to the new moment of suspension.

---

[18] Aided by high-speed photography, Dr. Holmström, a Swedish scientist, discovered that diagonal pairs of legs often do not strike the ground at the same time. He used the term "negative dissociation" when the front leg strikes the ground first and "positive dissociation" when the hind leg strikes the ground first.

Figure 4.23
The new moment of suspension.

Figure 4.24
The diagonal pair shows negative dissociation again; the left front hits before the right hind. The horse's left legs are on the ground and the right legs are raised, clearly a lateral canter stride.

horse is strong enough, or if the rider's methods are in other ways not classically correct, then the rhythm is the first casualty.

The rhythm deteriorates because the horse hurts, aches, and his muscles are strained. He may develop soundness problems. His attitude about work suffers. When he sees his rider, he thinks, "There is that person that works me too hard; the one that causes me pain." He develops tension in his back which causes the *losgelassenheit* to deteriorate. This is easiest to see in the walk, but symptoms occur at all of the gaits and even at the halt. Some people confuse a hot or overly energetic horse with a horse that suffers from being pushed too hard. A stressed horse with a lack of *losgelassenheit* is significantly different than a horse that is, by nature, nervous and easily frightened. Such a horse can spook and jump to the side, but he maintains an even, consistent rhythm in his gaits between spooks; the basic quality of the gaits is pure.

An important component of *losgelassenheit* is trust. A horse must trust his rider, and this trust is demonstrated at the halt and the walk. If a horse shows no halt, if the horse doesn't stand still for one second, then this horse should get a zero for this movement. If a horse shows a bad walk, one that is tense and has rhythm problems, then this is further evidence of deficiencies in the basics. And when the walk is gone, the horse is showing with only 1.5 gaits because half of the canter goes with it.

When these basics are not present, it is like having an opera singer who can only sing low notes. This is not a singer, at least not in the classical sense. Or it is the same as having a horse with three legs. Something very important is missing from the picture.

Instead of eliminating the walk from the Grand Prix, I believe that we should have more walk lessons. We should reintroduce the half pirouettes in the collected walk and the reinback-walk forward-reinback. Horses that have problems with *losgelassenheit* due to incorrect basics will also have problems with these exercises. People need to learn to appreciate the importance of a good walk.

When we depended upon horses for our livelihood, people had a better understanding of the horse's nature. Many years ago in Romania, my grandfather employed a young man by the name of Mr. Dichter. At that time he was about nineteen years old. I must have been about eleven or twelve years old. My grandfather had two horses that Mr. Dichter would hitch to a wagon for doing chores. Usually, Mr. Dichter would walk beside the wagon. I remember him always wearing a leather coat, and he carried a short stick with a short leather tassel attached. He used this as a whip. In the fall, one of Mr. Dichter's chores was to gather firewood for the coming winter. He took the horses and the wagon to a spot where they had cut down some trees for the community. I would often accompany him.

As Mr. Dichter walked off to lead the horses, he would swing the whip over his shoulder so the tassel hit the back of his coat. The popping noise from the whip was a signal for the horses to walk. I could see that Mr. Dichter loved these horses, and they returned his affection and trust. They would calmly follow him anywhere.

One day Mr. Dichter loaded the wagon a little too full. He failed to notice that the ground was damp from a prior storm. The wagon had sunk into the earth. An old farmer walked by and said, "Now, what are you going to do, boy? Your wagon looks a bit heavy."

Mr. Dichter quietly walked up to his horses. After giving them a pat, he turned, popped his whip on his leather coat and said, "Come on." The horses' muscles bulged under their harness and they followed. I stood amazed as the heavy wagon slowly rose as it left the damp ground. These horses trusted Mr. Dichter to be their friend.

Once again, I would like to make the point: horses need *losgelassenheit* to walk well. An important part of *losgelassenheit* is trust. We should always remember that horses are humanity's best friends. If they understand what we want and they are able, they will do it.

Figure 4.25–4.26

Watching Monica ride is like watching a swan glide across a pond on a breezy afternoon. The slight rhythmic motion that the swan absorbs from the gently lapping waves adds to the grace of the bird, which falters not once on its path. Monica floats across the arena in a half pass; the horse's feet are light and springy, which contrasts nicely with the ground-covering power from the hindquarters.

Her obvious passion for horses, whether inherited or absorbed from her father, is a key element of her talent. From this passion she forges a deep and trusting relationship with her mount. Harsh aids are unnecessary. Firm aids that quickly soften guide the wayward horse back onto the correct path. It is a well-established and ancient path that many have traveled before. A sense of peace and security prevail, born from a strong tradition of classical equitation.

The window into her relationship with her mount is the walk. Like the cowboy who crossed the desert or the farmer whose team pulled the plow, she is careful with this animal, lest she disturbs the rhythm of a quiet beat.

Nothing new is invented here. A wheel is still a wheel like a brush is a brush and a canvas is something upon which you paint. An artist can take the simplest of tools and create something that is both new and very old.

Training Questions

YOUNG HORSE

At what age should a horse be backed?

Horses should be started at age three or three and a half.

What is the most important thing when schooling a very young horse?

They have to learn just like I would teach a small child. They must be patiently educated and made familiar with things that will help with their future, like children.

What mistakes do you often observe?

The most common mistake is lack of patience. This causes horses to be pushed too hard.

Riders must spend time with their horses. This means not just when they are being ridden. We don't do this sport alone. Horses are not machines. We can't park them like a bicycle, or put them in the closet like skis. They are living beings. They have hearts. They are our friends. We have to allow them to occupy our time. This becomes a very rewarding experience.

What should the horse know at the end of the first year of training?

Regardless of the amount of natural talent in the horse, they need some time to develop at this young age. Some learn faster than others. It is important for their soundness—of mind and body—not to work them too hard. Horses need time to figure out their balance, to build the right muscles, and, most importantly, to develop trust. Trust is one of the first casualties of hurrying.

It is fascinating work when you think about it. You rebuild and rebalance the horse to carry a rider. You channel their natural instincts, reflexes, and thought processes to do our bidding. You build new muscles. This is a big responsibility. Horses need time to develop a consistent rhythm. I always look at the rhythm. Horses that are showing difficulty keeping a steady, unchanging rhythm while doing simple exercises need more time to get strong. You cannot force the rhythm into a young horse. You must patiently develop the muscles.

I'm working with a young horse now that has difficulty carrying himself in a nice, rhythmic trot. He has a very easy time in the canter, so we canter him more than we trot him. In the canter, we develop his hindquarters and make him stronger because he finds it easier. After he is stronger behind, he will also trot better. By doing what he finds easy, we also build his confidence. He has fun in his work. If we forced him to trot too much, his whole body would ache, and he wouldn't want to work.

Figure 4.27
Monica longes a young horse prior to mounting. "Longeing is a very good tool. It helps the horse to find its balance and develop muscles."

It is important with horses to carefully build their bodies and their minds. Then each year we see a little improvement.

When do you begin to train lateral work or the schools?

I don't like using leg-yielding. It puts the horse on the forehand. After the horses show that they can keep a steady rhythm and contact, when they understand moving forward from the leg a little bit, then they start to look supple and loose in their work. You can't say that this happens after six months or a year. It is difficult to put a timetable on it. When I see that they are loose and happy, that they are strong enough in their work, we try very few steps of moving sideways in a slight shoulder-fore. It is important not to do too many steps because the horse will get stiff and slow down. He will look cramped.

If a rider notices too late that the horse is uncomfortable, he can cause problems. Too late is wrong in dressage. The words *too much* and *too late* always mean that the person made a mistake. It is like pouring too much wine into a glass—a mistake. And it is also a very big mess if it is red wine. It is very important that the horse's work remains easy so he carries himself with confidence. Only in this manner can a rider train a horse that has fun in his work, a horse that wants to dance with his rider.

Figure 4.28
Lola shows nice bending through the length of her body. Monica's position is relaxed, with most of her weight on the inside. The horse travels uphill, with the poll at the highest point. The inside contact is soft and the horse steers from the legs of the rider. "I believe in riding outside with no rail. We place dressage letters in their proper positions, but we have no arena sides in between the letters. Consequently, riders must learn to use their outside leg to steer instead of the rail. The horse becomes more balanced and even in the contact." George Theodorescu.

Some horses, like some people, develop faster than others. Sometimes this is not an indicator of future talent. It is important not to work any horse too hard. You must take small steps. When I think of my riding, I feel that if I push for too much, it causes me to suffer a lot of anxiety, a sorrow that I have to live with. It is better not to ask for too much.

At what age do you begin to show horses?

Age three is a little young for me. I find nothing wrong with taking a four-year-old to a material class. They go around in a group at walk, trot, and canter for about five minutes. They get to experience the atmosphere at a show, the stabling, and the transportation to the show. They learn a lot from this. It's like

Figure 4.29

Monica Theodorescu riding Whisper during a clinic at the 2005 Global Dressage Forum. From this view of the shoulder-in, it is quite easy to see that the horse's inside hind steps under the center of gravity. This leg steps shorter and carries more weight. The rider's weight, which is positioned more over this leg, works in harmony with this process. The horse develops more power and engagement from stepping forward and under with the inside hind. Note that the horse's hind legs also remain close together, a sign that the rider has used enough outside leg to keep the horse's outside hind from swinging out. The outside hind leg pushes more and develops elasticity.

When a rider performs a shoulder-in as a lesson instead of a movement, the rider is able to teach the horse self-carriage. The rider is able to release his aids, and the horse does the shoulder-in without interference.

going to kindergarten with a kid. You take them by the hand and sing so they have some fun, so they are not frightened. The shows should be introduced along these lines.

COLLECTION

Do you use one form of lateral work more often than the others?

No, I use a mix of them all, shoulder-in, counter shoulder-in, travers, renvers, half pass. I use what I feel the horse needs, including the *volte* and large circles. These are all valuable lessons.

I vary what I do with each horse depending on the build of the horse. Do you write with the left or the right hand? When you ride a horse you must discover which side of the horse is dominant, where the horse is stiff and where he is supple. You vary your exercises to help the horse become more even in his body, more ambidextrous. But no horse is ever totally even. Even after many years of training, there is always a small difference between the two sides. The goal is to make them appear to be even.

shoulder back on my side that is closest to the rail. If I am on the left rein, I put my right hip and right shoulder back. I face the horse toward the rail and ride him sideways away from my leg on the outside of the arena. In this way I use the rail to keep him from running through my hands.

I don't think of working my horses hard. I think of using the lessons to teach the horse how to carry himself better.

What are common mistakes in the lateral work?

Most mistakes that I see have to do with the bending and the positioning. The horse has to bend throughout his body. In the shoulder-in and half pass, the inside hind leg of the horse must step under the horse's center of gravity so the leg carries weight. The rider must sit with less weight over the outside hind leg so this leg that has the longer distance to travel is not overly burdened.

This is especially true in the half pass. The inside hind leg must step under the center of gravity and step shorter, which is easier for the horse when the rider sits with more weight over this leg. If the rider sits with more weight over the outside hind, then this leg tends to step shorter and the half pass becomes more difficult for the horse; he can't pick up this leg and cross over the inside hind. When the rider sits properly, the horse lifts his feet in a light and springy way and the dance begins.

I see this mistake often in the Grand Prix. Riders change the half pass from one direction to the other, and they forget to change their weight. In the difficult trot half pass on the two short diagonals, this mistake has obvious consequences. The horse starts into the new half pass with the rider's weight on the wrong side. At first the horse tries hard to do what the rider wants, even though it is difficult. As the rider nears the end of the diagonal, the horse is tired, and the rhythm starts to suffer.

Figure 4.30
Monica introduces the half pass to Lola. From this angle it is easiest to see that this young horse keeps stepping forward with her legs; too much shortening would be immediately visible. A young horse should step forward and only a little sideways with a small amount of bend. If the rider tries to get too much crossing of the legs or bends the horse too much, the rhythm will suffer. When you introduce half pass, you should ride like you only have judges at B and E.

Note that Monica has turned her right hip and right shoulder back slightly. Her weight is more on the right seat bone.

George Theodorescu said, "When I watch this mare, Lola, work, it makes me wish I were young again. She has a natural rhythm and a powerful hind leg. As she develops her carrying power, the true beauty of her gaits will emerge under the weight of a rider. This process cannot be hurried. You cannot force a horse to carry more weight on the hindquarters if the strength is not there. Riders who force horses too quickly cause rhythm faults. Usually the rhythm in the walk goes first. When that happens, half of the canter rhythm goes with it. Now the horse is traveling on one and a half gaits."

Which combinations of lateral work do you prefer?

I do not have combinations that I prefer over the others. I vary the combinations according to the situation. For example, if I have a horse that likes to pull when I ask him to go sideways, I'll ride him in the indoor and use counter shoulder-in. I turn my hip and

Figures 4.31–4.32
There is an obvious difference between the engagement and power in the five-year-old horse (above) and seven-year-old (opposite). Developing this power takes knowledge, time, and patience.

This also happens in the canter zigzag. The rider doesn't change his weight, and he interferes with the gaits of the horse. The horse is unable to perform a flying change of lead. A rider should always think about returning to a neutral position after each movement. At the end of a half pass or even a shoulder-in, he rides straight, in this neutral position. In this way each lesson has a beginning and an end. He must not ride into the next lesson until this neutral position has been obtained.

When is a horse ready to collect?

From the first moment when a rider sits on a horse, the training toward collection begins. The horse starts to learn simple exercises to take more weight on the hind legs. This is the purpose behind the half halts and the transitions.

But even on simple exercises like a circle, one hind leg comes more under the center of gravity, and the other hind leg must step longer and push more. With some very young horses, you can see problems if the rider tries to ride too many circles. The horse starts to labor and loses the rhythm. Riders on such horses should change direction often, from one big circle to the next so the horse doesn't get too tired.

When the horse is somewhat more advanced, I use counter canter and serpentines in the canter. Counter canter is a great straightening and engaging exercise. My riders don't collect through the hands and spurs, we collect through the exercises. In the right canter, the horse's right hind carries more weight, and the left hind pushes more. If I ride counter canter on a serpentine on a bent line, then the carrying leg, the right hind, comes under the horse more. A rider should ride this exercise forward, like a hand gallop, and not try to collect the horse too much. Sometimes riders resort to draw reins or double bridles to try to pull the horse back. The rider should ride forward and let the exercise collect the horse.

When do you start to train flying changes?

I start to train flying changes after the canter is somewhat collected. However, before I try to ride flying changes, I start with simple changes. The horse learns to go from one canter to the next with a few walk steps in between. Through this, the horse learns to change his balance from one lead to the next.

It is important to ride quietly in the simple changes. Even these changes have their rhythm. The horse must not anticipate the new lead so much that the walk suffers.

How do you usually train changes? Which figures and lines do you use?

I use straight lines, a short diagonal, and serpentines. If I use serpentines, I ride big loops, and I first ride a simple change when I change direction. The horse must stay quiet. It is very important that the horse does not get too tense. I half halt to prepare the transition and then walk. I change the positioning of the horse and then canter. The rider must remember that the horse has four legs and it takes time to reposition the horse. If the rider is not patient, the horse gets tense and doesn't learn as easily. The rider must be one with his horse.

I repeat the simple changes a few times. It is important to remember to place your weight over the correct leg. Once again the rule of always having your weight over the hind leg that is most under the horse plays an important role; lighten your weight over the leg that has the farthest distance to travel. After a few of these simple changes, I do the same thing without walking, and the horse performs the flying change. If you ride this correctly, you can soon do the changes with the reins in one hand because the horse understands what you want. Basically speaking, this is not a difficult lesson. But if the rider has not prepared the horse properly, or if he makes mistakes with the aids, he should never blame the horse.

When is a horse ready to learn piaffe?

The piaffe starts with the collection. As soon as horses begin to learn the collected trot, they are learning in the direction of piaffe. Through the half halts the horse learns to bring his hind legs more under his center of gravity, one of the key steps in learning piaffe.

One of the best preparatory exercises for piaffe is to ride trot-halt-trot transitions. The rider first prepares the horse for the halt with several half halts. Of course, the rider must strive to ride with invisible aids and maintain a nice, even rhythm during this preparation. At the correct moment, when the horse is soft and ready, the rider asks for the halt. After standing immobile, the rider closes the leg and asks the horse to trot. When the horse can strike off from the halt to the trot by lifting a diagonal pair of legs, not walking or shuffling his legs, then the horse is starting to understand the piaffe.

What other techniques do you use to begin to train this exercise?

Of course, I work horses in hand. Horses learn this exercise easier without the weight of a rider. I also use a steep hill on my property. When horses walk down a hill, they close their hind legs under their bodies. This is a good time to ask for the piaffe.

One of the most important things for trainers to remember when they teach this difficult exercise is that they must effectively communicate with the horse. They shouldn't rely too much on the spurs or the whip to get horses to piaffe. Horses are very willing when they understand what the rider wants them to do. Also, some horses have more talent than others for this difficult movement.

I once had a five-year-old mare that had super talent for piaffe. At that time my wife had a gelding that she was teaching to piaffe. I would ride next to her with my reins in one hand and help her by sometimes tapping gently her horse's croup with my whip. After a few days her horse started to get the idea; he began to do some nice half steps.

That's when my wife looked over at my mare and said, "Look, she has learned to piaffe too."

I laughed and patted the mare. Sure enough, she had learned by watching the other horse learn. This mare really had a lot of talent.

When is a horse ready to passage?

Once again, like the piaffe, the horse learns to passage from the collected trot. When a horse is supple and loose, he can travel with sufficient impulsion in the collected trot. The horse will start to offer passage when the rider uses proper half halts. If the basics are correct, then horses have an easy time understanding this lesson. Just like in the piaffe, some horses will passage better than others, but most can learn a little passage.

How do you train this exercise?

One method I use is similar to the piaffe exercise. I trot then halt a few times. Then I use the half halt and prepare the horse to halt, but instead of halting, I add a little impulsion with my driving aids. Usually, the horse will offer a few passage steps. This is enough. I reward the horse.

Do you teach piaffe or passage first?

When I start training piaffe, I usually start teaching passage also. When the horses are ready for one, they are ready for the other.

What are some common mistakes?

Often, I see unevenness. The horses do not maintain a regular rhythm. Another common mistake is that the horses lower their heads instead of their haunches. By definition, a horse in the piaffe should lower and engage the haunches. A horse that fails to do this is not piaffing. Sometimes I see that the horse's tail end is higher than its withers. If the rider turned around in the saddle, he would be riding an uphill horse. This happens often with riders that train their horses in a very deep frame. Many times these riders use draw reins to pull the horse's head down between its legs. This is against the natural tendencies and conformation of the horse.

I'm fairly certain that the horse is the only animal in the world that looks man in the eye. An elephant's eye is very high, and so is the giraffe's. The lion, king of the beasts, runs around with his eyes next to the ground. The horse stands proud next to us, as a friend, and looks us right in the eye. To pull his head down is degrading, to force it between his legs.

Draw reins are not allowed to be used at my barn.

What do you wish that you would see more often?

I wish that I would see more horses be even in the piaffe. Many horses do not lift their legs in even diagonal pairs; they lift one pair higher than the other which causes an irregularity. This comes from mistakes in the basic training. The horse has not been ridden straight or the horse has been pushed too hard. Horses must be ridden calm, straight, and forward. When Steinbrecht said in his time that people should ride their horses forward, people understood what he meant. Perhaps in our time we should add *always, always, always* forward. A lot of crookedness in horses comes from people riding backwards and using too much hand.

Circus trainers often have problems with irregularities. I have nothing against circus trainers, quite the opposite. Most are talented and have very good relationships with their horses. But their job is difficult because their presentation must take place in a very small arena; so they train in this small arena. Most horses are not ridden forward in a large open area. The trainer's job is to show

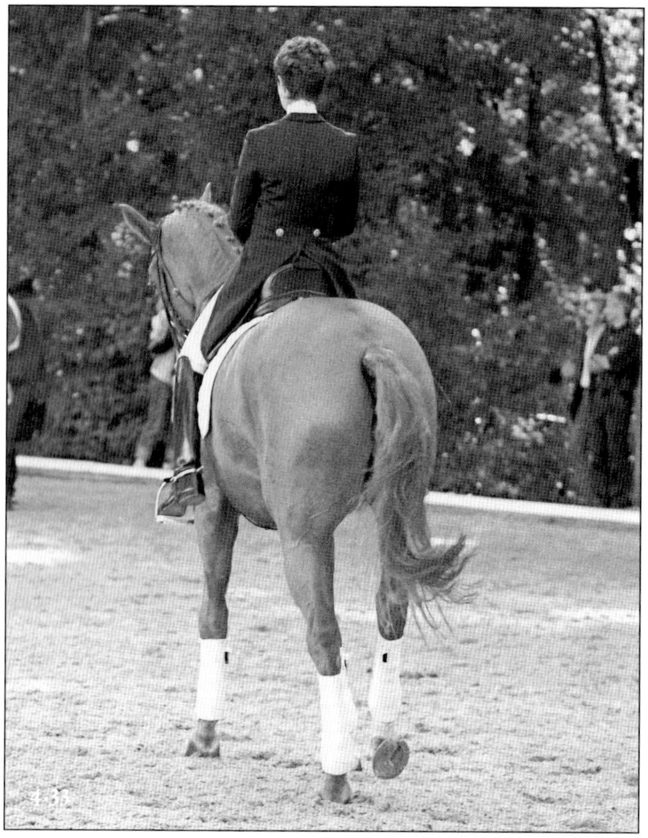
4.33

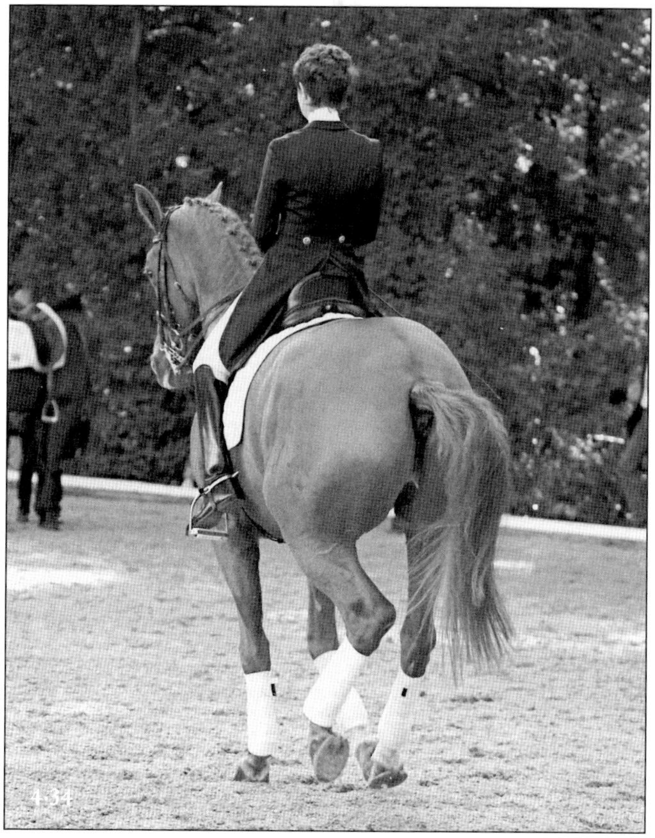
4.34

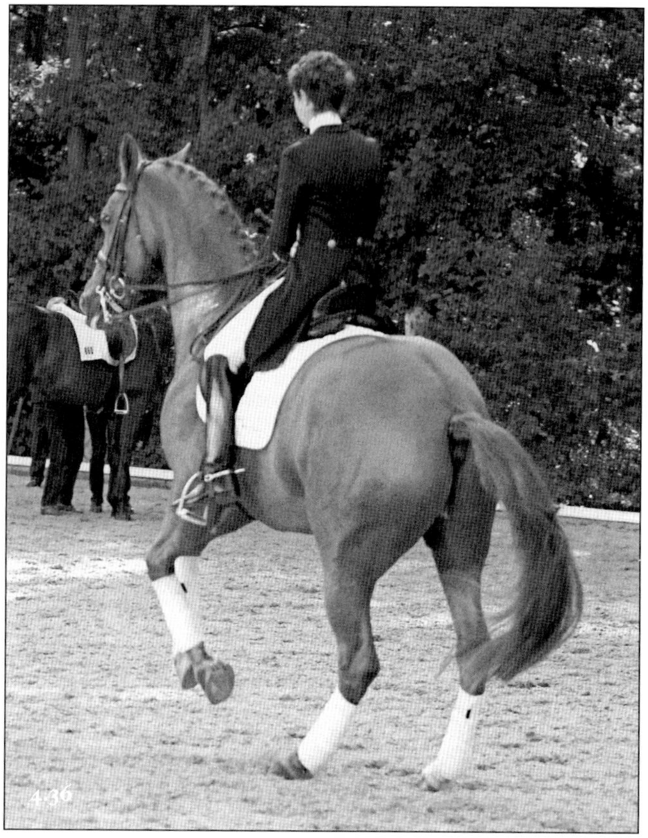
4.36

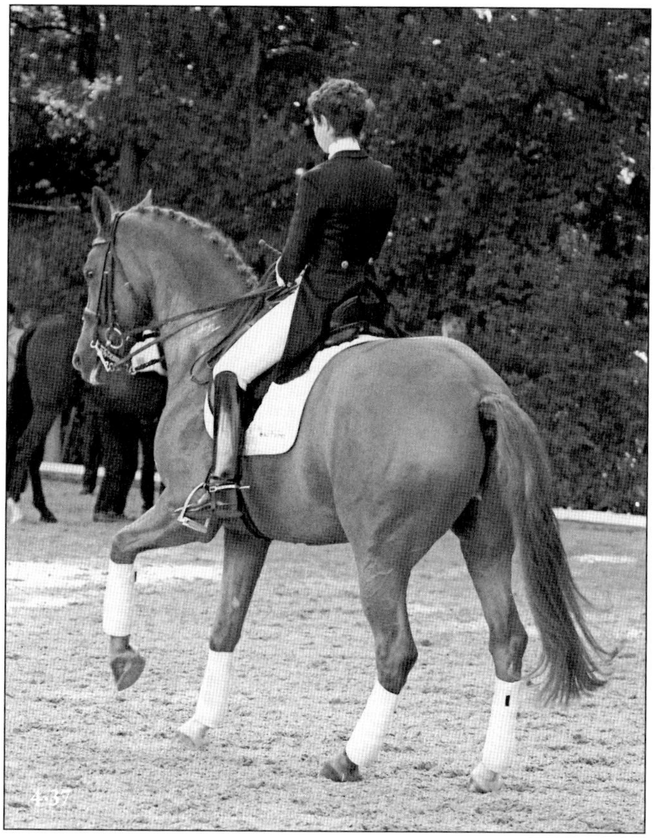
4.37

Figures 4.33–4.48

"The horse has to be balanced with the rider's lower back in the pirouette. When I ride a pirouette, I can release my reins, and the horse will not run forward." George Theodorescu.

Monica Theodorescu rides the pirouette in an uphill canter with the poll as the highest point. Her position enables the horse to step under with activity as he turns his front end around the hind end.

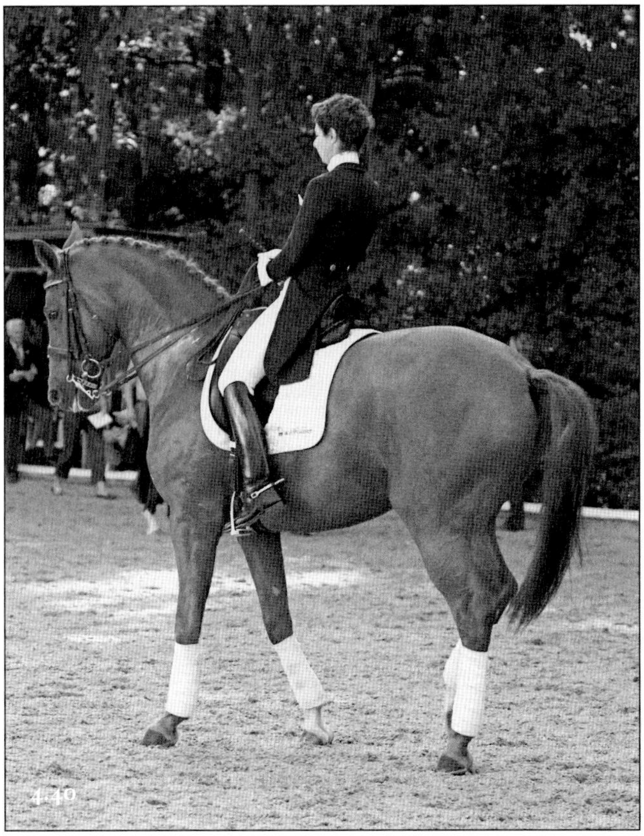
4.40

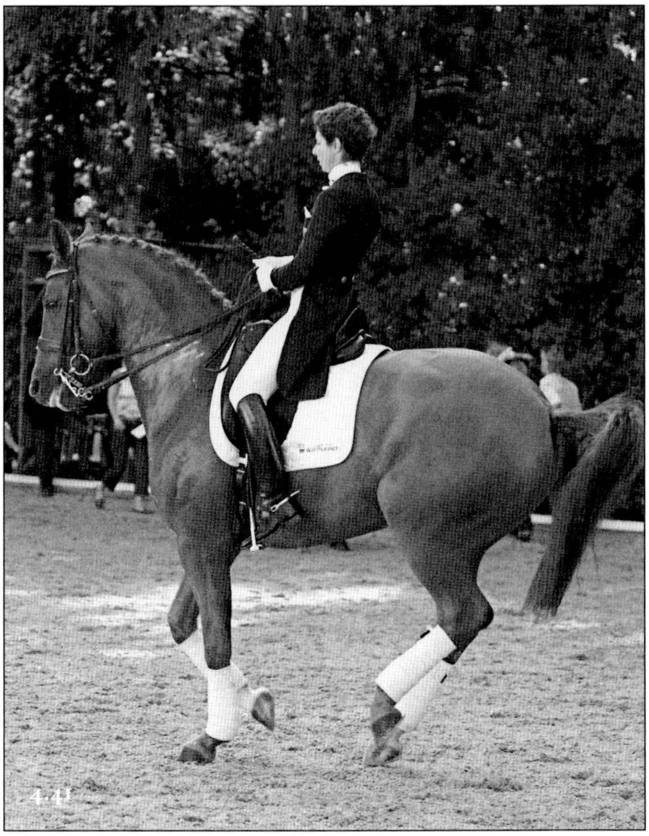
4.41

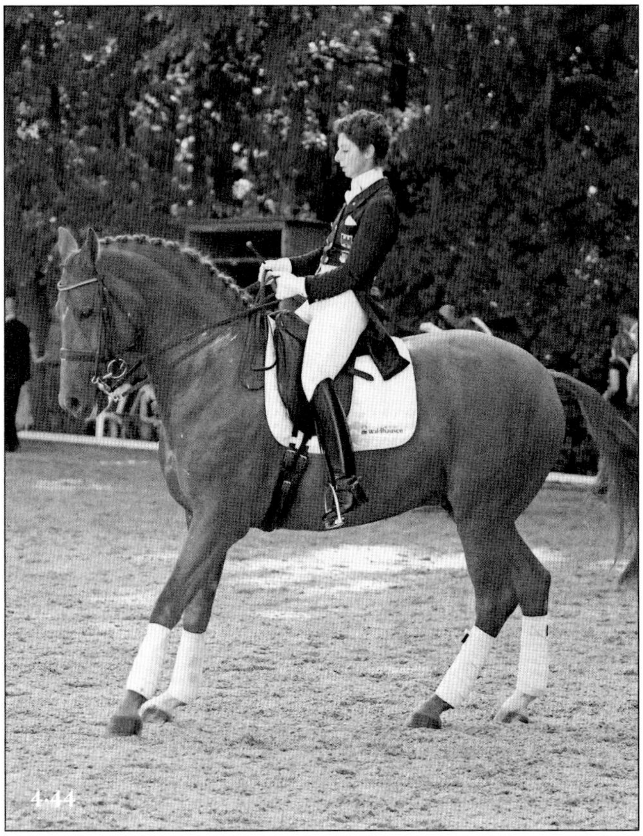
4.44

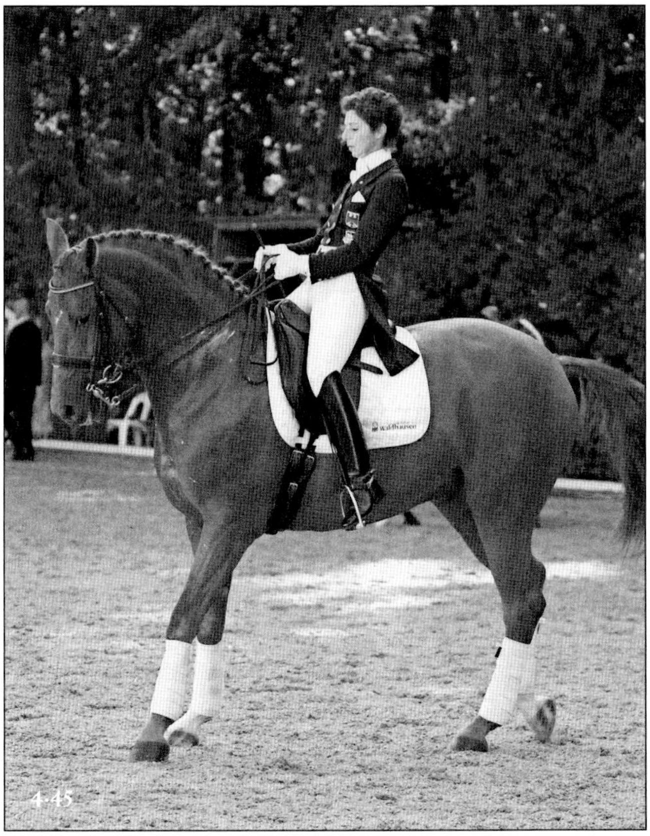
4.45

4-42

4-43

4-46

4-47

must canter uphill with his haunches lower and reach up and out with his legs. Gradually the horse learns to canter more and more on the spot.

What are some common mistakes?

Often the horse will not keep enough impulsion in the canter or they will lose the uphill frame. Sometimes they spin too fast, and the rider loses control of the rhythm.

Many riders will over-ride the pirouette. Sometimes I hear trainers telling their students to ride more forward. I think ride more forward—where? You are supposed to be cantering on the spot; if you ride forward, you will no longer be doing a pirouette. The student who rides too forward will also have to hold too much to keep the horse from cantering away. The horse will be confused and thinking, "Should I, or shouldn't I? What is wrong with my friend? What does he want?" This starts a bad cycle. The rider must learn to half halt properly and to keep the energy in the pirouette.

something spectacular for the audience in a tight space. But if you watch the circus trainers closely, they always have something in their pockets for the horses, and the horses know this. The horses look happy.

A rider who trains in a large area but doesn't train forward can create these problems without the small arena. By using too much hand and riding backwards, he makes the horse uneven or irregular.

What do you wish that you would see more often?

The rider must have the horse balanced by using his lower back and interacting with the motion of the horse. In a pirouette the horse must canter on the spot. I can ride a pirouette and give forward with both hands, and the horse will stay on the spot and jump in a nice, even rhythm. My hands are not keeping the horse in the pirouette.

How do you train pirouettes?

I usually start by spiraling in while riding the horse forward in the canter. As the circles get smaller, so do the strides of the horse. I use half halts to encourage this. But it is important that the horse maintains a regular, even canter with plenty of jump. The horse

How would you describe a perfect half halt?

When you can't see what the rider did. You see a reaction in the horse from invisible aids.

Figure 4.49
George Theodorescu pictured during a clinic at the 2005 Global Dressage Forum.

Which mistakes do you often see with half halts?

Often the riders are too hard in the hands. The half halt is also an exercise to prepare the horse. For example, if the rider wants to halt, he should half halt, half halt, and then halt. The rider shouldn't surprise the horse with a sudden and strong aid. Again, we have to come back to the point that the rider has two legs and the horse has four. The rider must learn patience and to prepare the horse for movements with half halts and not expect immediate reactions from strong aids. Eventually the rider and horse can learn to half halt with invisible aids and halt with invisible aids.

Figure 4.50

Note Monica Theodorescu's relaxed expression. Harmony comes through relaxation. The *losgelassenheit* of the horse comes from the *losgelasenheit* of the rider. During the Global Dressage Forum, Monica said, "Once after watching me school one of my horses at home, a guest asked me, 'When do you ride dressage?' She saw me practicing serpentines, transitions, half halts, and then more serpentines at the trot and canter. I told her that I don't ride movements every day. My horse knew the changes. If there were to be a mistake, it would be my fault, not the horse's. The same concept was true for the other lessons. On a daily basis, I keep the work simple and basic. I only practice more of the lessons before a show."